From the
Summer of Love
to the
Valley of the Moon

— A Memoir —

Nancy J. Martin

Contents

✌

✌

Harpo's Blues

— Phoebe Snow —

I wish I was a willow
And I could sway to the music in the wind
And I wish I was a lover
I wouldn't need my costumes and pretend
I wish I was a mountain
I'd pass boldly through the clouds and never end
I wish I was a soft refrain
When the lights were out I'd play
And be your friend
I strut and fret my hour upon the stage
The hour is up
I have to run and hide my rage
I'm lost again
I think I'm really scared
I won't be back at all this time
And have my deepest secrets shared

I'd like to be a willow
A lover, a mountain or a soft refrain
But I'd hate to be a grown-up
And have to try to bear my life in pain

The Prophecy

Walking the gangplank onto the entrance of Juanita's Galley, a nasty combination of fish and septic gagged me, cutting through the scent of my musk oil. This was the night after my mother threatened me — "Don't ever let me hear that you've been to Juanita's. It has the worst reputation in the San Francisco Bay Area and you'll never live it down!" Naturally I could hardly wait to get there and check it out. Inside, the air was thick with smoke, reeking of booze and patchouli. What a scene.

It was 1966 and I was eighteen-year-old Nancy Tindell, still innocent but rebellious as hell. My much more worldly new friend Bonnie and I had our weekend all planned. Bonnie was a pretty, petite sex pistol, born for trouble. Her new boyfriend Kelly was a drummer with the Marin County band, Morning Glory and booked to play at Juanita's on Saturday night. We arrived with our long, dark, shiny, parted-down-the-middle hair wearing vividly colored mini-dresses, knee-high black leather boots, and sparkly love beads. Bonnie's hair was chocolate brown and straight as a stick. I envied her Joan Baez look. Mine was long, dark and curly-wavy. I would lay it over an ironing board and take a hot iron to it to get the look I wanted. All night we alternately got high in the bathroom or danced our asses off to the band's screaming-loud mesmerizing, psychedelic sounds. Bonnie was snorting speed. Who knows where she got it? This penchant for the hard stuff would be her ultimate undoing.

The club owner, Juanita Musson was a bona fide character.

She easily weighed 250 lbs., had long gray hair, huge pendulous boobs and a loud brassy voice. Juanita would greet her guests sprawled on her large, untidy bed. A pet monkey scampering around would nip at you if you got too close. Every patron had to pass the bed for her inspection, which was stationed near the entry of her houseboat-nightclub floating on Sausalito's Richardson Bay.

Kelly brought his friend Al Strong to our table during the band break. Al was the bass player in the *Sons of Champlin*, another Marin rock band that was making the scene around the Bay Area. According to Al, we originally met late one night at the Red Kettle, a funky diner on the canal in San Rafael where Bonnie and Kelly introduced us. Al was cute, funny and a few years older than me. That night at Juanita's he was dressed in a cool paisley shirt, strings of love beads and soft, brown leather, handmade boots. The guys in his band called him "Fuzzy," because he had shoulder-length, light-brown hair and a huge fluffy mustache. When the band began their set Bill Champlin, the bandleader introduced Fuzzy to the audience. Al came out to the edge of the stage and did a crazy little comedic dance. He was hilarious, eliciting laughter and applause. We hung out together all night. Before long we were a steady item, and my life as I'd previously known it was at an end. My new hippie lifestyle would become the bane of my mother's existence.

It was my good fortune to have been born an only child in San Francisco to the unlikely pairing of an Eastern European Jewish mother and a Southern Baptist father. My mother's family of four boys and two girls came from New York to sunny California, settling in the little Sonoma County town of Petaluma to raise chickens on a rural farm. My father proudly told stories about growing up in a large family in Oklahoma, when it was still Osage Indian Territory. His father, of English and Scottish origins, was a circuit-riding Southern Baptist preacher. He rode horseback through Arkansas and Oklahoma, preaching fire and brimstone to those unfortunate souls whose towns were lacking a brick and mortar church. My grandfather claimed to have once been locked in a shed by the Jesse James gang, who didn't want to harm a preacher, while they were busy robbing the local bank.

On my mother Lillian's side, the Epstein family produced ten first cousins at the end of World War II including me. Her entire family put down roots around the San Francisco Bay. All of the cousins were unusually close-knit as children and have remained so into adulthood. My father John's family, the Tindells, lived mostly in Texas and Arkansas. Dad didn't keep in close touch, and I never had the opportunity to get to know them. His father the preacher had been a violent man and my father went to live with his high school principal when he was fifteen. When Dad graduated, the principal gave him a train ticket to California to seek his fortune. He established a management career with Piggly Wiggly stores, later purchased by Safeway, then enlisted in the Navy. Not long after the war ended my folks met at the USO in San Francisco, where my mother was serving donuts and hot coffee to the returning veterans. He followed her home on the bus and the rest is history.

San Francisco, true to its famous mystique, was constantly foggy and damp, especially out on the avenues, not known for balmy climes. As a child I had chronic ear infections and tonsillitis. When I was nine, our doctor recommended more moderate temperatures for me as a cure. As a result, we moved to northern Marin County where the weather was warm throughout much of the year. My dad bit the bullet and commuted down Highway 101 every day, crossing the Golden Gate Bridge to operate his liquor store in San Francisco. Mom was the perfect 1950's housewife, cooking and planting flowers in her garden, always an active member of the PTA. She got involved in local hot-button causes anywhere she could find a home for her highly opinionated personality. Unfortunately, this tendency manifested itself in extremely harsh, judgmental forms, alienating both my father and myself. Mother had unrealistically high expectations of me. She made it clear throughout my life that anything I did or achieved was not good enough. I walked on eggshells around her. Growing up in this tense atmosphere took an early toll on my self-esteem.

Reading books stands out as one of my earliest childhood memories. Mom, an avid reader herself, would take me to the library and let me pick out books. I discovered as soon as I could read that it was a pleasant way to transport myself to another realm. I began reading books and newspapers in kindergarten. When we relocated across the bridge to northern Marin County, I was placed in fourth grade, skipped from the low third class I had been attending in the city, basically skipping an entire year. Labeled "precocious" based on my reading ability, I became the youngest child in my class and eventually the youngest in my high school graduation class. This early reading comprehension became my foundation for a lifetime goal of clear communication.

Our comfortable house in a rural Novato subdivision was situated across the street from designated open space woodland. Natural springs and creeks bubbled up in the tall grasses, where colorful wildflowers bloomed and kids could play. It was an ideal place for a child to grow up. Dad owned horses throughout his life and loved to ride. As soon as my feet could reach the stirrups, he would take me to riding stables where we rented horses and rode out into the hills together. I can still recall the sound of his beautiful barbershop-quartet trained voice singing..."water, coool water." Horses, riding, horse husbandry and spending time in nature quickly became a touchstone in my life. The greens of nature became my favorite colors. I drew horses, played horses, collected horse statuary, and at age nine I was presented with my first real, live, horse. Maggie was a Standardbred who had been a trotter on the track. She was a beautiful, fast bay mare who won each time I challenged anyone to a race.

On Christmas morning in 1958, I opened a large, colorfully wrapped box, which contained my first Western saddle, a beauty that served me well into my adulthood. Every second that I was not in school was spent with my horse and I considered myself to be the luckiest little cowgirl in the world.

A common question for parents today is, "Do you know where your kids are?" In my pre-teen years mine seemed fairly unconcerned, knowing that I was out having fun with Maggie. During summer vacations, my mother would often drop me off at the boarding stables to ride in the mornings. Dressed in my jeans and cowboy boots, carrying a sack lunch, I always started out clean and by the time she picked me up in the evening I would be filthy after a day of riding. This was my escape from my father's drinking and my mother's subsequent, constant rage. Allowed the freedom to go off alone, I eventually became fearless and free, riding Maggie all the way to San Rafael, or up into the mountains of northern Marin without the help of maps. I always found my way back before dark when it was time to feed my horse. I learned to deal with barbed wire, ranch gates, wildlife, and the occasional accident on my own.

I rode in local equine play-days and participated in the annual summer Novato Western Weekend parades decked out in my entirely purple outfit, accessorized with a violet neck scarf, boot covers, hatband, and my big sterling silver belt buckle. Once a year we would hitch up the horse to an old-fashioned black buggy with red wooden wheels, which we cleaned up like a shiny new penny, and listened to applause all along the parade route of our main street. Participating in the annual Western Weekend Parade was a real thrill for me. Keeping and loving horses became a lifetime passion, helping to mold me into the person I was to become.

As the years passed, I became an uncomfortable child in the middle of my parent's ongoing arguments. They used me like a ping-pong ball, each guilt-tripping me to side with the other. When I was 10, sitting in his Nash Rambler, listening to Elvis crooning "Don't Be Cruel," my dad told me that he would divorce my mother if it were not for me. This was depressing and confusing for a youngster, instilling sad feelings I have never been able to shrug off. I always made friends and did fine in school, but was unhappy and used the freedom I enjoyed with Maggie as a release from tension. Even today, when asked about my love of spending time in the saddle, I say, "Well, it's cheaper than a shrink."

My first job, at age 11, after obtaining my childcare badge in Girl Scouts was babysitting. One of the mothers whose children were put into my young care happened to be a fabulous seamstress, and she taught me to sew. Taking me along with her to purchase sewing supplies initiated my lifetime fascination with fabric stores and color. I began to make many of my own clothes when I was fourteen. Holding up my latest creation for my mother's approval, she would invariably remark, "that seam is crooked," or "you could do better." In lieu of expectations, this was my lesson simply to do my best work and keep my business to myself.

In addition to drawing horses on my school notebook, I obsessively began to design dresses and suits, dreaming that I would grow up to be a famous clothing designer. During my high school years, I was an Avon Lady, walking door-to-door wearing a pink linen hand-tailored suit of my own making. Selling cosmetics was easy. Housewives welcomed me into their homes to test my samples. I won a diamond Avon pin, presented to me at a local hotel, for best salesperson in the area. The hardworking, adult Avon Ladies in attendance that day were not thrilled when a fifteen-year-old girl won the coveted pin! Many years later, Joe Martin, the boss and super salesman at St. Francis winery who would later become my husband, told me, "Nancy, you could sell snowballs to Eskimos."

My first proposal came when I was no more than twelve years old. This seems to have been a quirky omen to my doomed marriages. A teenaged neighborhood boy named Lucky proposed marriage while we were sitting on the curb one Saturday morning in front of my house. I can't remember

Lucky's face and don't remember my reply, but what I do remember, is him going into our house to ask my father for my hand in marriage. My dad flipped out and threatened poor Lucky's life. Dad saw no humor in this youthful fantasy. That was the last time I was allowed to hang out with Lucky. Each time I see a movie depicting a father holding his shotgun while greeting his daughter's date at the door, I remember that summer afternoon.

Later, when I was about fourteen, I met a boy named Dennis at the rodeo. It was love at first sight. Dennis was a handsome boy with dark wavy hair and his cowboy boots were always spit-shined. We would sit on my back porch in the shade for hours rubbing saddle soap onto our saddles and boots. Somehow we found ways to make riding dates, even though he went to Novato High and I was at San Rafael and my mother was still driving me around. Dennis came from a good family and my parents thought that our puppy love was pretty cute. It was all completely innocent of course, however he did offer me his undying love. When his heifer calved he named it Nancy.

My first serious kiss was delivered by a young cowboy named Larry, up under the rafters of an old barn, in a dusty hayloft, just like in the movies. This relationship was short-lived. I was jailbait.

––––––––––

In my junior year at San Rafael High my best friend Derrith was a platinum-haired girl a year ahead of me in school. We were inseparable and were known at school as "the blonde and the brunette." I spent many nights sleeping over at her house in San Rafael. Derrith was raised as a practicing Mormon. Her mother, father, and older sister were kind, respectful and loving toward me. Since I felt entirely misunderstood and disrespected at home, I loved spending time at Derrith's house. No one in her family ever suggested that I should go to church with them, tried to convert me, or even spoke much about their religion. I do remember though, when leaving on our customary double dates, Derrith's mom would always quietly tell us at the door, "Remember who you are." This made a big impression on me. We were still innocent; virginal and carefree. This was 1964 and I was fifteen.

At sixteen I was old enough to get a driver's license. Dad taught me to drive, and made sure I knew how to change a tire by myself before handing over the keys to my mom's old car. My new acquisition was seriously ugly; an extra-long, four-door 1958 Plymouth Belvedere, sporting hideous salmon paint and humongous tail fins. It was embarrassing, but definitely beat riding the school bus. Every morning I picked up a load of neighborhood girls and we whooped it up all the way to school, smoking cigarettes, rolling up our skirts and putting on way too much makeup. I had to put a quart of oil in that old Plymouth every day, but it ran and was my next stepping-stone to freedom and away from my squabbling parents.

Derrith went off to BYU when I became a senior. I had a terrible falling-out with my parents. I can't really say that I ran away from home but I announced that I was leaving, packed up my stuff into the old Plymouth, and moved onto a houseboat in Sausalito with an older girl who rented me a room.

My parents didn't try to stop me. I think that they were relieved to see me go.

This was the height of bohemianism...the beatnik life. I bought my first pair of knee-high, butter-soft, black boots in a very hip, below-the-sidewalk mod shop in Sausalito. My new look included wearing turtleneck sweaters, parting my elbow-length hair down the middle, and smoking cigarettes. I loved the freedom, didn't mind being broke and still continued to drive myself to San Rafael High every day. Some of the activities from my high school days that continue to influence me included jewelry-making and pottery classes taught by the volatile and inspiring Mr. Moezzi. In Mr. Curtin's humanities class we explored art history as well as a basic study of Buddhism, which turned out to be a theological epiphany for me. I was also a staff member writing for the school newspaper, The Red and White, mentored by our much loved and very hip Mr. Langton. One of the great perks from working on the newspaper was my hall pass, which allowed me to get out of or be late for classes to cover a story. I could go sit under the bleachers on the football field and smoke a cigarette, imagining myself becoming a widely read journalist. One of the kids also working on the newspaper was my good friend Jim Kilgore who, shockingly, later joined the Symbionese Liberation Army (SLA) and became one of America's Most Wanted Men. But in 1965, Jim was one of the sweetest boys in school. Not a boyfriend, but a good buddy. In our 1965 school yearbook, The Searchlight, Jim filled an entire page in my book inscribing, *To Nancy, My dear skipping and handholding partner in Journalism. I'll never skip with another. Jimmy (blue eyes) Kilgore.*

I spent much of my senior year palling around with my friend Linda, another blonde with big blue eyes. The boys were crazy about her. I began to spend a lot of time at her home in San Rafael where her parents allowed us a kind of liberty not offered to me at home. We would cruise up and down 4th Street in San Rafael for hours — a la American Graffiti — hanging out and looking for parties. We are good friends to this day. I graduated at age sixteen, by some miracle still a virgin.

My steady boyfriend, Bob, attended Tamalpais High School in Mill Valley. This was hands-down the hippest school in Marin. All of the black kids from Marin City attended school there, including the brilliant jazz pianist George Duke, who was in Bob's graduating class. We listened to a lot of jazz as well as rock and roll and double-dated with black couples, a fact that would have caused my Southern father to put me on restriction and sequestered in my room for the rest of my life. But this is where I really learned to dance and also developed a lifelong addiction to straight-ahead jazz.

Derrith had been away at Brigham Young University for a year. We wrote regularly, she extolling the beauty of Provo, Utah and the charms of the university. She begged me to come. At this point my parents would have done anything to pull me out of what they considered the depths of hell. BYU accepted me for enrollment and I naively allowed my parents to sell my horses, pack me up and drive me to Provo where I was exuberantly welcomed by Derrith and her housemates. If I thought that I had been unhappy before, this was to be the bitter, unsweetened dark chocolate icing on my cake.

Naturally, the school administration was bound and determined to convert every "non-Mormon" student, as they referred to us unconverted types. At first I was well accepted by the other students and was rapidly streamlined into one of the most popular girls' organizations called Sportswomen. Sororities and fraternities were not allowed. I went out on dates with hunky, preppy Mormon guys and tried to fit in, but this lifestyle was not my cup of tea. In 1965-1966 when I attended school there, The Beatles became a huge worldwide musical success. That same year BYU banned rock and roll music from the campus on the grounds that "it was carnal." The daily, relentless attempts at conversion, and mandatory *Book of Mormon* classes were just too much for me. I had a Jewish mother, a Southern Baptist father and was cultivating a strong interest in Buddhism. I was on religion overload; I left at the end of the school year with a poor excuse for an academic record.

Returning to my parents' home was yet another shock. My mother wanted to monitor me and was critical of my every thought, word and deed. We were constantly at loggerheads. I dutifully enrolled in the College of Marin, got a job and soon found an apartment in the hills of Fairfax, where my roommate Bonnie concentrated on teaching me the fine art of partying. We were both pursued by local guys and had endless fun. Then Bonnie met Kelly, drummer for the band *Morning Glory* and I started dating Al, the bass player in the *Sons of Champlin*. Bonnie and Kelly got married. Bonnie was nineteen and I was eighteen.

A Product
of My Environment

My new life began in the time directly following the infamous summer of love. It was 1967 in Marin County, just minutes away from the Golden Gate, which led directly to the corner of Haight and Ashbury. I was simply a product of my environment. I was working in a local bookstore, earning a fair wage at a nice job, living in the Fairfax apartment and driving a very cute little forest green MGA I had paid for myself — which elicited a fair amount of attention wherever it took me. When I was nineteen Al and I decided to get married. The *Sons of Champlin*, who had morphed out of their previous band called *The Opposite Six*, often performed as the back-up band for groups like *Dick and Dee-Dee* and the *Righteous Brothers*, at the Corte Madera Rec Center and the Santa Venetia Veteran's Hall. The band was managed by a man named Frank Werber. Frank also owned the infamous Trident Restaurant located on the edge of Richardson bay right on the main drag in Sausalito. He was also involved with Capitol Records and had his own music company, Trident Records. Jazz greats such as the *Denny Zeitlin Trio*, which included Dr. Zeitlin on piano, the great Charlie Hayden on bass and Jerry Granelli on drums had recorded on the Trident label and often played at the Trident. We were living in Sausalito and decided to get married. Frank generously offered to foot the bill with a local artisan jeweler who created beautiful custom gold wedding bands for us and as if that were not enough, he paid to have handcrafted sandals made for us to wear at our wedding.

Mine laced all the way up to my knees in soft brown leather. I loved those sandals and wore them for many years. We were the epitome of a cool Marin County hippie couple. When we married I was nineteen and Al was twenty-two. We had a rock and roll wedding, held outdoors at the Muir Beach Overlook where everyone would be free to smoke all of the pot that they desired before, during and after the ceremony. I designed and made my own ivory lace wedding dress and a matching Indian shirt for Al. The entire band joined us, as well as many of the *Sons* constant entourage and of course, both sets of our parents. The photos clearly show my mother completely dressed in black, as for a funeral. She brought a many-tiered wedding cake, which to her horror, tumbled into pieces on the way up the mountain. She was in tears the entire time and not, may I add, were those tears of joy. My mom was horrified. It was 1967, I was a nineteen-year-old, married, college dropout and my mother's prophecy had come true. I will always remember how, as my father walked me down the path leading to the minister, he whispered over and over into my ear, "It's not too late. You can still call this off."

Soon, as Al's new old lady, I began going with the band to all of their gigs at places like the Avalon Ballroom, Chet Helms' Family Dog out on the Pacific Coast Highway, Bill Graham's Fillmore Auditorium, and Winterland — where Al remembers with some embarrassment, opening a show for the *Grateful Dead* with the *Sons* all dressed in pajamas. The band played every nightclub and concert venue around the bay. To get to these gigs all of us, players, wives and girlfriends, along with all of the instruments and equipment, packed into the open back of Bill Champlin's beat-up white van, with Charlie Kelly, the band roadie at the wheel. There were five guys in the band. Bill Champlin wrote much of the material, was the lead singer and was also competent to play almost all of the instruments. His primary instruments were piano, his big B3 organ and he often played a mean rhythm guitar. Terry Haggarty was the wild and talented lead guitar player. My husband Al played bass with his buddy Bill Bowen on drums as the rhythm section and Tim Cain the sax player. This was the original core of the group when I first met them. Al, Tim and Hag had become friends at Sir Francis Drake High School in San Anselmo, where they all had participated in the school music department and played in a band called *The Starlighters*. Bill had married his high school sweetheart Elaine, at a young age and they had a toddler son, Brad. Later, Jeff Palmer, the immensely talented musician who played alto sax and vibes had come out from the East Coast with his friend Jim Beem the trumpeter. Now the band had a big horn sound like *Coldblood* from the East Bay and *Chicago* — a band that Bill Champlin eventually joined.

The *Sons of Champlin* met Fred Roth, a charismatic, curly haired guy who was working the light show at the Fillmore Auditorium. Fred was a photographer who liked their sound and expressed interest in photographing the band. Later, Fred and his lady-friend Ann Hatch, basically adopted all of us. We were perpetually starving kids and began spending a lot of time at their enchanted cottage high up on Mt. Tamalpais, perennially encased in the fog. We typically spent many nights of the week there, eating dinner and getting stoned, while Ann cooked countless pots of brown rice for us and Fred took photos. Fred managed the band through the recording of the first two LPs; *Loosen up Naturally* and the *Sons*. He had a friend named Ron who was managing the legendary San Francisco rock band, the *Quicksilver Messenger Service*. The *Sons* began to open many shows for Quicksilver. Eventually, Wally Haas — who had become a good friend of the band — took over the reins as band manager and *Follow Your Heart* became the third and final Capitol Records recording for the band.

Because the *Sons* opened shows multiple nights a week it would not be uncommon to find us sitting around in a grungy dressing room, smoking joints and drinking with the likes of Janis Joplin and her band *Big Brother and the Holding Company, Charlie Musselwhite, The Jefferson Airplane, Elvin Bishop, Nick Gravenites or Maria Mauldaur and the Jim Kweskin Jug Band*, locals like us, but also folks like Paul Butterfield, BB King, Albert King, *The Young Rascals, The Grateful Dead*, and Joe Cocker, etc. There were just too many acts to remember, or as we used to say, "If you can remember then you probably weren't there." Al tells some humorous stories about the time the band backed Chuck Berry in Denver, Chuck stopping in mid-act to give Al a hug. Or the time that they opened for Chuck, but his bass player didn't show up and so Bill Champlin — who was not a bass player — stepped right up and played bass with Berry's band, or the night they opened for *MC5* in Detroit, and got busted and Tim Cain had to play the drums because Bowen and Palmer had been detained by the authorities. One night I saw an incredible live show with Jimi Hendrix and *Cream*. I watched in horror as Jimi smashed his guitar into a zillion electrically charged pieces onto the stage and my thought was — "...Oh how disrespectful to his instrument" — followed by the great power trio *Cream*, with Eric Clapton, Ginger Baker and Jack Bruce, a mind-blowing finish to that show! One Thanksgiving evening, the *Sons* had a gig at Winterland. Al and I went around to various doors and no one would believe that he was in the band that was opening the show. They didn't hand out ID tags in those days and finally, Al demanded to see Bill Graham, who eventually came to the door, pissed off as usual, and let us in. Naturally, we were hungry, it was Thanksgiving. We went backstage and saw a long table laden with luscious foods. As we wandered in we were quickly and none too kindly ushered out by Albert Grossman, the manager for *The Band*, the most famous band of all, Bob Dylan's band. The food was, of course, all for them. We were so jealous. But the show was fabulous and unforgettable, even though Bob was not there that night.

Did I mention the groupies? OMG. There was a reason why everyone used the term, "sex, drugs and rock & roll." Each band had an entourage who followed them to every show. Within each of those adoring groups were the uninhibited, sexy young girls dressed in feather boas and sheer dresses. They would throw their panties up onto the stage in hopes of being invited backstage to be involved in whatever might be happening at that moment. Many of these young ladies were not particularly discerning as to the outcome of their panty throwing. They would gladly schtup the roadie behind a speaker box, as end up with one of the band members just to be able to boast that they were personally involved with the group. It was a time of free love and no bad vibes.

For this job each guy in the *Sons* received ten dollars per week pay, which was intended to cover our total expenses including groceries and gas. This meant feeding maybe ten guys and their ladies and transporting them. Management paid the house and rehearsal space rents and utilities and supplied us with all of the grass that we could possibly smoke. Some of the band members and their ladies lived and had their babies in tents. Sometimes we didn't have much to eat, but there was always lots of pot. We were too stoned to care. On most days the gas money had to get us all to gigs and to The Sausalito Heliport, which rented out rehearsal spaces to numerous cool Bay Area bands. On any given day we could wander around the huge heliport and listen to great bands like *The Electric Flag*, rehearsing their acts.

We had been happily married for a couple of years when I became pregnant. I was overjoyed and Al too was very happy at the thought of becoming a father. We were sharing a house in Lagunitas, in the San Geronimo Valley, with Tim, his girlfriend Pam and the various people who came and went, crashing there when they needed a place to sleep or something to eat. I had begun to experience pain, which I naively attributed to the pregnancy and started to spend more time in bed. It was actually considered cool at that time to receive visits from friends while lounging naked in bed, after John and Yoko had released their own photos showing them hanging out in their bed. One day feeling bored, I went along to the heliport for rehearsal. I was sitting on the floor, leaning up against Bill's big B3 organ speaker and the next thing I remember was waking up in Marin General Hospital. The medical staff had given me a spinal injection and told me that I was experiencing an ectopic pregnancy. The fetus had become lodged inside the fallopian tube and had begun to grow inside of the tube. My fallopian tube had burst. I was fully awake when the doctor said, "Oh look, it's a boy. Do you want to see him?" They subsequently removed all of my female organs on the affected side and kept me hospitalized for a couple of weeks, informing me that I would no longer be able to bear children.

We lived like gypsies in various rental houses, out in rural West Marin. This was a secluded and magical valley, which is situated between Fairfax and Point Reyes, a good place to get lost. I found an adorable little white cottage in Lagunitas, right on the edge of Samuel P. Taylor State Park. Bonnie and Kelly lived right next door. The back of the property bordered a running creek and it had a fruit orchard. I had been given a flashy, dappled buckskin Arabian mare with a white mane and tail, named Shalizar. As the story went the poor horse had previously been owned by a crazy dope dealer, who had given her LSD. As a result, she would spook at every falling leaf and had thrown off and injured a number of both men and women. The unfortunate horse had been passed around hand-to-hand and finally ended up behind my house in the orchard. I babied her, we got along fine and she never gave me any trouble. Although I still owned my childhood saddle, I usually rode Shalizar bareback. From our house I could ride all day long, up into some of the most scenic and remote areas imaginable, boasting huge crystal clear lakes and giant stands of redwood trees. I was in heaven. One day, while riding around a secluded lake with my waist-length hair blowing in the wind and shirtless in the sun, I remember startling a lone fisherman as we came around the edge of the lake. I'm guessing now that this is a vision he wouldn't soon forget.

The *Sons* had released their LP, *Sing Me A Rainbow* and were out on the road touring much of the time. Their song, *Get High*, was a big hit and they were attracting a lot of attention. Al came home from a tour feeling pretty pumped up and informed me that he now wanted to have an open marriage with two wives. I was working at a local health food store and as always was involved in creating and selling my art. I was quite independent on my own and didn't take kindly to his suggestion. My first divorce was quickly forthcoming, too late for Al's remorse.

Trouble
In Paradise

The times they were a changin' for me. Finding myself suddenly single and free was a bit of a shocker as I had been a happy, monogamous young wife and now all of the margins of my life had been thrown wide open. This was a time of introspection, fun and freedom. I remember driving alone, high up onto Mt. Tamalpais in Mill Valley, on my way to a nude be-in. All of the beautiful long-haired, unself-conscious young men and women there were quietly picnicking and socializing in an exquisitely bucolic and secluded setting on the mountain, entirely in the nude. Many of us wore handmade, colorful love beads, hats or scarves but not much else. The atmosphere was peaceful and quiet — good vibes, baby.

Ever the artisan, I was very involved in the art of spinning wool on my spinning wheel. Hiking up through verdant folds of the rolling Marin hills I collected bark, flowers and plants that I brought home and cooked up, creating dyes of every hue and tone from nature. I had taken a class at College of Marin, learning the fine points of this process and the results were absolutely brilliant. In addition, I was creating original, designer leather clothing made from the softest deerskins, which I purchased at a tannery. On my hikes I would also bring home huge, many-pointed antlers shed by wild bucks. These I would cut, polish and make into beautiful buttons, which would adorn my deerskin handbags or fringed jackets. Always I managed to earn enough money by creating art to supplement the income from my various jobs to make myself comfortable. One summer I took my spinning wheel and equipment to the Renaissance Faire in Marin, camping there with the other Faire-goers. Early each morning, I set up boiling pots of water for dyes, demonstrating the dying process for the many Faire visitors during the day, endlessly spinning and dying yarn. It was a fabulous fantasy life that lasted only a week but has remained a fond memory.

Still, I carried on as usual, working at the health food store in Forest Knolls, gardening, creating my art, riding my horse and walking many miles a day, even though I owned a vehicle. I had moved into a rustic rental house owned by my boss Richard, which was located on a fire trail, high up on the Woodacre ridge. Often I would walk, instead of driving, down the fire trail and all the way to Forest Knolls where I worked and back again at night. Having no fear of the dark, I loved the hike back up the mountain trail, lit only by the moon and the stars. The house was quite secluded, located deep in the forest and had room for a large horse corral, which held Shalizar and a cute little chestnut mare named Misty, who belonged to my friend Mark. From my house I could ride endlessly, either up into the mountains or down into the valley.

One day I rode Shalizar from home, down deeper toward the valley floor of Forest Knolls. Coming over a knoll, I spotted a guy with long auburn hair sitting outside on a deck, beating on his practice pad with drumsticks. He waved, I waved back and without stopping, Shalizar and I continued on our way. Within the next couple of days that same auburn-haired guy showed up on my doorstep, having asked around about me. He said that his name was Bill Vitt and that he had an interest in leasing a horse for riding. I actually believed him! Misty's owner, Mark, had asked me to find someone to take responsibility for her financial care as he was back and forth to Southern CA. This seemed like an easy solution. I took Bill and Misty out on one trail ride — and somehow at the end of that day he just never left. Bill moved into my house a few days later. He also never got on Misty again. I was more than astonished when Bill told me he had just been hired as the new drummer for the *Sons of Champlin*. The band had let Al and Bill Bowen go. So I morphed right back into the band, as Bill's old lady, minus the communal living. We needed the privacy. This was a big love, much more intense than anything I had ever experienced before. My body was quickly awakening from its youthful languor. Bill told my neighbor Donna that it was, "… like out of True Romance Magazine." He was working regularly with the *Sons*, Merl Saunders and as an in-demand studio musician on various recording projects and we were financially sound. He was often away and I never gave it a thought because we were so happy and I was, as usual, the love-blinded, trusting, monogamous young woman.

Getting to know Bill, I learned that he was actually a professional, wage-earning studio musician with an extensive list of credits. In 1970 he and his friend John Kahn had played on *Brewer and Shipley's* album *Tarkio*, which had a number one hit with *One Toke Over The Line*. Bill's performing and recording career also included work with the *Michael Bloomfield Band (Electric Flag), Sons of Champlin, Tom Fogerty[1] — Creedence Clearwater Revival, Pee Wee Ellis, Ivan Neville, Sonny and Cher, Freddie King, the Coasters, James Cotton, Charlie Musselwhite, Chris Hayes — Huey Lewis & the News, Nick Daniels — Dumpstaphunk, Neville Brothers, Eddie Harris, Tony Saunders, Billy Connors — Chic Corea, Felton Cruise — Miles Davis), Eydie Gorme* and probably more than I've listed here. I'll have to admit that I was impressed. He was handsome and talented.

Bill was spending a lot of time working and recording with the *Jerry Garcia/Merl Saunders band* (1970–1975), Jerry Garcia[2] (vocals, guitar), Merl Saunders[3] (keyboards), John Kahn[4] (bass) and Bill Vitt[5] (drums). The legendary Live at Keystone

---

[1] Tom Fogarty: November 9, 1941–September 6, 1990
[2] Jerry Garcia: August 1, 1942–August 9, 1995
[3] Merl Saunders: February 14, 1934– October 24, 2008
[4] John Kahn: June 13, 1947–May 30, 1996
[5] Bill Vitt: May 6, 1943 –July 19, 2019

recordings were made at this time. He was also doing a lot of gigs with *Mitch Woods and his Red Hot Mama — now Mitch Woods and his Rocket 88's.*

Hanging out with Merl and his family at their home in the city, was always a treat. Chronically good-natured, grinning ear-to-ear with his big gap-toothed grin and wearing his ubiquitous black leather fisherman's cap, Merl was everyone's favorite daddy. He literally exuded love and his music and performance exemplified his sweetness. He always made me feel loved and welcome wherever we were. His obituary in *SF Gate* called Merl, "…the gentle lion of the SF music scene…"

John Kahn, his beautiful blond wife Deidre and their adorable toddler son Jaime lived in Forest Knolls, not far from our place in Woodacre. Bill and John were known as a rhythm section team in the rock music world and were close friends. I got along well with John and quickly became close friends with Dee. One night when Bill was working in the city with Mitch, the Kahns invited me to a dinner party at their home. Dee was a great cook and everyone was having a typical 70's blast. At one point I left the table. Walking back to my seat, I felt myself roughly grabbed, and pulled with two forceful arms down into the lap of Michael Pollard — CW Moss of *Bonnie & Clyde* — one of the dinner guests. Michael was laughing hysterically, but I didn't think that it was funny and asked him, "Who do you think you are?" — which really pissed him off.

In 1972 we were offered the opportunity to rent a very nice house at Nick's Cove, in Marshall, right on the water's edge, a stone's throw from Hog Island, now a popular oyster farm. West Marin is paradise, but the Inverness, Pt. Reyes, Marshall and Tomales areas around Tomales Bay, are especially spectacular. Having always enjoyed my privacy, I was very happy to be living on the water with unlimited miles to walk. Bill was commuting the coastal roads to Fantasy Studios in Berkeley every day in our très cool silver Karmann Ghia. Tom Fogarty — *Creedence Clearwater Revival* — had hired the Garcia/Saunders band to back him on a couple of albums (*Tom Fogarty and*

Excalibur). Hanging out in the studio at Fantasy was a lot of fun.

Things seemingly went along fine for a couple of years when, much to my surprise, I learned that I was pregnant. Bill had always been a serious, daily beer-drinker and pot smoker and I never thought much about it. However — sadly enough — by the time I was several months along into the pregnancy, he had become a full-fledged, needle-using junkie. This was a game-changer for me. In my naivety, I had not realized that all along he had also been having one-night stands with many other women. My obviously pregnant state did not elicit the kindness or respect a pregnant woman would expect of the father of her child. Instead he became more and more addicted and with that came less interest in the baby and me. I was very unhappy, completely devastated and confused.

I had been working for the better part of a year, in a really great job as a secretary at The Monster Company, owned by Stanley Mouse and his business partner Alton Kelley.[6] This was my happy refuge, a place where I felt useful, productive and appreciated. It was also a very hip and cool art studio, more of an art hub really, where all of the local San Francisco Bay Area poster artists came and went. Victor Moscoso, Pat Ryan, Wes Wilson, Rick Griffin and many of the artists who did the (now iconic) handbills and posters for the Avalon and the Fillmore hung out there. It was a fun and supercharged artistic environment. Together, Kelley and Stanley created many of these art pieces, which are now collector's items. It was fun to watch them, sitting with their airbrushes, left-handed Kelley and right-handed Stanley painting together on the same piece. The Monster Company revolutionized and set the standard for silk-screened art t-shirts. Stanley and Kelley personally created the many designs t-shirt designs such as zigzag man, skull & roses, the ice cream kid, gypsy woman, and the vintage car series. *Rolling Stone Magazine* ran regular ads for the Monster and

---

6 Alton Kelley June 17, 1940 — June 1, 2008

orders poured in. It was my job to fill the orders. I worked there while I was pregnant with my daughter and happily came back to work following the pregnancy.

Returning to the valley from Marshall, we had rented a storybook cottage on yet another fire trail in Woodacre, down closer to the valley floor. It could not be reached by cars, which were parked at the bottom of steep steps, made from railroad ties, always slippery from the constant moisture of the forest and the overhanging giant green ferns. At the top of the steps stood an adorable and secluded little white cottage, completely encircled within a grove of giant redwood trees. It was a fairyland beyond compare; the ever-present fresh scent of the forest could take your breath away. The cottage also had an outdoor, redwood deck where we slept beneath our redwoods in the summers. If this sounds like heaven, it was, excepting for the sordid fact that Bill was a junkie. One night at home, I got a call from Bill telling me that his car had broken down on the Miracle Mile in San Rafael, asking me to come pick him up and take him to work at a club in the city. It was a stormy January night and I was heavily eight months pregnant. I dutifully walked down those wet slippery stairs in the dark, which led to my parked car at the bottom and drove to San Rafael to go collect him. When I found him, soaked on the side of the road, he climbed into my car and pushed me over to the passenger side. Reaching across to open the car door, he literally threw me out onto the cold, rain-soaked street and quickly drove away before I could even get up off of the ground. It was raining hard and I had no rain gear or proper shoes for the weather. There I was, pregnant and standing in the rain, in the dark on a busy street, so I stuck my thumb out and waited for someone to take pity on me and give me a ride. The man who eventually pulled over was absolutely horrified at my condition and instead of threatening, harming or molesting me, insisted on taking me all the way back to Woodacre. This was indicative of the peace and love mindset of those times. Soaked, crying and hysterical I called my friend Deidre. She was livid as I tearfully related the story and came right over to get me.

Driving straight to the city, we arrived at the club where Bill and John were working that night with Mitch Woods. Dee marched right up to the bar and ordered a glass of beer. She walked up onto the stage as the band played, throwing the beer right in Bill's face, soaking his hair, clothes and drum set. He did not miss a beat and the band played on as we walked out of the club.

Our healthy miracle, baby daughter Aura Serena arrived early in the AM on February 22, 1974. My plan was to have the baby at home. I was three weeks past my due date on Merl's birthday, which happened to fall on Valentine's Day. I really wanted to have the baby that day, so nine months and three weeks into my pregnancy, I jogged to the bottom of the fire trail and hiked back up in hopes that it would induce labor. No such luck. It had already been arranged that my OB-GYN would come with his nurse when I went into labor. Little did he know that he would have to walk up through the forest in the moonlight to find my house. As was the custom with home births then, select friends and family members were invited to be present. My parents, completely unprepared for what was to transpire, made their first visit to our little house replete with a huge deli platter to share as if heading out to a party. As always, my friends Bonnie and Kelly were there to support me. Nudity has never been an issue with me and as Bonnie walked my naked, pregnant self around between rounds of intense contractions, my parents were more than stunned. Back in the day when a woman was in labor, the father was asked to step out of the room. These days, the medical community frowns upon both going past due dates and prolonged birthing times but in 1974 we just waited it out. After twenty-four hours had passed with me beginning to show some worse for wear, the doctor much to his credit for hanging in there with me, now had second thoughts about attending home births and later confessed to me that it had been the most "traumatic event" in his entire medical career. Deep into the night everyone, including my exhausted parents, walked me down those treacherous, slippery steps under the giant redwoods, down to a car and drove me to Marin General Hospital — where Bill passed out on top of me in the delivery room and was escorted out. This was not a big surprise to me as he had also fainted during the film at the one Lamaze class he had grudgingly agreed to attend. None too soon, I finally gave birth. Having refused all offers of drugs since the onset of labor, this was agonizing for all concerned but was worth it in the end. The baby arrived completely awake with her little brown eyes wide open. My father was overjoyed and insisted until the day he died that Aura had looked directly into his eyes the minute that she was born.

During this age of rock & roll that had swept the nation and also the world, many of the rock bands were using drugs such as meth and cocaine and the sound of their music reflected that state of mind. The *Sons*, on the other hand, were primarily pot smokers. Pot, although illegal, was cheap and it was often given freely to all of us. There was no violence associated with marijuana then. Many people fooled around with psychedelic drugs, but a few of the guys in the *Sons* became obsessive about them and were seemingly forever negatively affected by the residual effects of these mind-altering drugs. The band had visited the then-famous hippie commune in Southern California, The Hog Farm. They returned back to Marin with a huge burlap bag full of peyote buttons. These small cactus buttons contained the psychoactive hallucinogen mescaline, widely used by various Native American tribes for the purpose of seeing visions. The huge burlap bag was deposited in a corner of my kitchen in Lagunitas for communal use and we all gave it a try. The unpleasant thing about peyote consumption was its emetic effect. The taste is revolting and as a result the body, in its attempt to reject it, experiences vomiting prior to the resulting psychedelic experience. Nevertheless, we used up every last button in milkshakes and peyote pancakes, which I made by the dozens for our many friends that kept my blender whirring.

Heroin, however, was a different story, not producing the ubiquitous munchies or happy giggling effects brought on by pot smoking. Instead, going without creates violent sickness. This does not make for a happy person. Using junk causes extreme but brief euphoria and then the user passes out — going on the nod — basically creating a zombie whose only mission in life is to obsessively obtain more so that they can do it again. My daughter's father had become a different person, lethargic, mean and completely self-centered.

One day while I was in the kitchen, with baby Aura crawling at my feet, Bill who now carried a gun, suddenly put a kitchen knife to my throat. Erratically pushing me up against the sink he said, "I'm going to take this baby and you'll never see her again." Naturally I was terrified. Really scary and crazy people were coming and going — in and out of the house — buying and selling drugs, guns and other things. Immediately I began to devise a plan to get away to save our lives, to take the baby and leave as soon as I could possibly arrange it. My only thought, akin to that of a mother bear, was the natural instinct to protect my young. Bill had been traveling more and more, which was fine with me as I was now done with him. I had my own income and felt much safer when he was out of town. I started seeing a friend of Bill's, named David, who was very good to me and who loved Aura. David wanted to get married. We had a lot of fun together, but this was very sudden and I hedged.

Rain On
My Parade

Shopping one day in Fairfax, I was introduced to (the late) Michael Barclay. I was very attracted to him, but was not pleased to discover that he was a musician. Michael was a guitar player who had recently arrived from the East Coast with his keyboard-player buddy, Ozzie. They had come to Marin in hopes of aligning themselves with the San Francisco music scene and had befriended some members of the Jessie Collin Young band, who were living in West Marin. Although I was still seeing David, I also began a feverish love affair with Michael who was well aware of my plan to relocate. Michael was an eastern educated, preppy guy from a very good family who had lived and raised their three children in Westchester, NY. He was disillusioned with his upscale eastern upbringing and was very excited to be on his own in California, playing music. Many of the local musicians were friendly, sitting in on each other's gigs to jam. This is how Michael got to know Bill and Bill knew that I was seeing Michael.

Aura was a year old, walking and already talking. On the day of our departure to Vancouver, Michael drove the baby and me to the train station in Oakland. My parents were there to see us off. This is what I remember: Sitting on a bench in the train station, holding Aura on my lap, with Michael sitting on one side of us, and David on the other. My poor mother, more confused than ever by my non-conformist lifestyle said to me, "You've told me about David, but who is this other man?" I said that I intended to marry him.

A few of my friends had relocated to Canada for various reasons and I contacted all of them, asking if they would help me in starting a new life if I were to come to Vancouver. The responses I received were surprisingly open, positive and welcoming. Now, when people ask me how I made and implemented my escape plan I have to say that it was literally dumb luck. I applied for a new id, got a copy of my birth certificate, bought a train ticket to Vancouver, packed up things for me and baby Aura and left. In short, I became at the same time an expat and an illegal alien. In order to qualify for landed immigrant status in Canada, one needed to show proof of secure financial backing, which I could not prove. Also, the Canadian government was quite strict in its laws governing work. They absolutely would not allow a non-Canadian to take a job that a Canadian could fill. Luckily for me, my friends would soon be opening a nightclub/restaurant in Vancouver and had offered me a job waiting tables for which I would be paid in cash. In the interim I found a very cozy, light and airy, furnished apartment on the second story of a lovely older home with a large yard, where Aura could play. It was located in a very nice neighborhood, not far from where I would be working. Fully aware that I was living the life of an outlaw was very frightening to a young mother alone in a foreign country. I am reminded of this today on a daily basis, as frightened immigrants stream into the US from all over the world in an attempt to save themselves and their children from harm.

Michael was sending me love letters, filled with hopes and ideas for the future. He insisted that his wish was to marry me and adopt Aura and said that he would be coming for a visit as soon as possible. I would count the days. Vancouver was a stunningly beautiful and vibrant city with clean air, lovely architecture and charming neighborhoods. The diverse international population was sophisticated and fascinating. The city was packed with reasonably priced, multi-cultural bistros and cafes, as well as fabulous upscale, white-tablecloth restaurants in every neighborhood. East Indian, Native American, and European food was available at all times of the day and night, at prices that fit my budget. It was springtime and the weather was perfect. Gardens filled with brilliantly colored flowers bloomed all over the city. The baby loved to play with her toys on the green lawn, safely enclosed by a classic white picket fence.

Construction on the nightclub was finally completed. A wildly successful grand opening party brought in crowds from all over the city. Every night the club was packed to overflowing with Canadians eating, drinking and dancing to the hip Canadian rock groups that were booked in every night. I came to work in the afternoon and worked until closing at 2AM, hiring a babysitter to stay with Aura until I got home. Little Aura woke up early each morning. A lack of sleep left me tired but happy to be able to spend time with my daughter during her waking hours.

Earning the means to pay my rent and care for the two of us allowed me to feel very independent, yet I was also very sad to find myself a single mother. I had fled Marin, wishing to get as far away from the local drug culture as I could, leaving Bill no notification or information about where I had gone. Michael was doing a good job of keeping my whereabouts a secret, sharing it only with my parents. To my extreme delight and surprise, my mother wrote to tell me that he had come to visit them at their home and had actually asked my father for my hand in marriage. My mother was absolutely smitten with Michael — his blond good looks and nice manners. She was over the moon at the prospect of our impending marriage and the likelihood that we would return to Marin, where she hoped we would establish a normal life. Spring had rolled into a wet and chilly fall in Vancouver. Our amorous correspondence continued. The months passed very slowly until the day that Michael finally arrived. He had quit his job as a ski repairman in a sporting goods store, sold most of his belongings, bought a big white van and driven to Vancouver with his white German Shepherd dog.

I will always remember sitting in the warm sun on the lawn in our flower-filled yard, playing with the baby and suddenly seeing him come through the gate. It was for me as if the gates of heaven had opened. I was delirious with joy. Michael moved into my apartment, planning to stay as long as the Canadian government would allow his visa to continue. He sat in regularly with the various bands playing at the club and on nights when he wasn't playing music, he was able to stay at home with Aura while I worked until 2AM — a huge relief for me.

Working long hours combined with a lack of sleep left me continuously exhausted, but very contented in our little family and Michael's promise of commitment to us. Little Aura and Michael — who ultimately became Dad — bonded quickly. Michael acted toward her in the responsible and protective manner of any good parent. Not having actually married Aura's father, would now allow my life and new plans to proceed in a much simpler manner. Eventually Bill showed up, asking me to marry him, claiming that he had "cleaned up his act and was a new man," but I couldn't forget the frightening memories and didn't trust that things would actually be different if I were to marry him. When he arrived, I told him that I planned to marry Michael. Within twenty-four hours Bill had flown his latest girlfriend there to be with him, invalidating everything that he had said to me. That cinched the deal.

Weeks stretched into months in Vancouver and then Michael received notification that his tourist visa was about to expire and would not qualify for renewal. We were forced to make some serious decisions that would affect the entire remainder of our lives. Both of us had friends and connections living in the San Francisco Bay Area. My old friends Bonnie and Kelly, as well as my old flame David — with whom I had maintained a close friendship — were both living in the little town of Sonoma, not far from my parent's home in Novato. Sonoma seemed like a quiet and homey choice for a place to begin our new life together and a good place to raise a child. Both of my folks had become realtors in Marin and after doing some research they found a funky little farmhouse with a huge backyard with the very low rent we could afford. We thanked all of our Canadian friends who had helped both of us transition through a very difficult time, packed up everything we owned into Michael's white van and drove back over the border heading into an unknown future.

We had very little money, but at least my parents had paid for a few months of rent, until we could get on our feet financially. Michael went back to his job at the sporting goods store and I found a job waiting tables at the old historic El Dorado Hotel, on the plaza in Sonoma. It had a bar and a huge dining room, where the food was served in traditional Italian family style. This meant carrying large bowls of minestrone soup and numerous courses to each table. Backed by its many years of Sonoma history, the food at the El Dorado was notoriously good and the work was hard. Aura was 2 years old, a typically active and adorable toddler, talking a blue streak. Again I was working at night and in the morning I was on mom duty until it was time for me to go back to work. In between, my friend Bonnie occasionally watched Aura, who loved to play with Bonnie and Kelly's little daughter Raven. It was easy to fall in love with Sonoma, a sleepy little town tucked in a verdant valley between Napa and Santa Rosa, with its charming historic plaza and quaint eastside neighborhood. We were married in 1976 in the corner, west-facing second-floor judge's chambers, in the old stone city hall — which remains today located in the center of the Sonoma Plaza. Michael's friends Ozzie and Ruby joined us as witnesses and I wore my long, brightly colored, hand-embroidered Afghani wedding dress. We were asked to wait in the anteroom outside of the judge's chambers where, much to our horror, prisoners in shackles having just been sentenced were led out and we were invited in. Not an auspicious omen! Following the ceremony, the judge proceeded to deliver a severe lecture to Michael regarding the sacred nature of marriage — the judge must have had a clue. We all thought it was pretty funny at the time. Now in retrospect, I have to wonder.

People jokingly referred to Sonoma as "Slownoma." There was not much nightlife in our little burg, other than a movie at the stately old Sebastiani Theatre on the plaza, following local Mexican food and margaritas. Michael would drive to Marin or the city to play music. He had been hired to play guitar in the *Merle Saunders Band* and was scheduled to go out on tour to back the soulful jazz and blues singer Randy Crawford. Randy recently had a big hit with the venerable *Jazz Crusaders*, vocalizing *Nightlife*. This was a very big opportunity for Michael and he was thrilled. Out on the road for a number of weeks, he would call home to check in and describe to me what was happening on the tour. As the only Caucasian person in the band, he was taking a lot of teasing. But he said that the music was great and he was enjoying the touring experience. Meanwhile, life went on in Sonoma for Aura and me. Our large, quiet back yard had plenty of room for Aura to run and play while I worked in the big vegetable garden I had planted, right next to a huge leafy fig tree. The historic old town of Sonoma sits in the base of the Valley of the Moon, sheltered on one side by picturesque Sonoma Mountain and on the other separating Sonoma from Napa Valley, the Mayacamas range. The majority of the historic district surrounding the plaza is flat and perfect for walking. Quiet streets bordered by charming homes, completed the picture of serenity. Each day I would put Aura in her stroller and walk for miles, enjoying the perfect weather and lovely surroundings. We had chosen the perfect spot to call home.

Michael had left his job at the sporting goods store and was beginning to teach guitar lessons for income to supplement whatever money he could make playing music. He always had a band for local gigs and wanted to include me as a female singer. I loved to sing at home and in the car with the radio, but had paralyzing stage fright in public. This was a fiasco, and to my chagrin and Michael's disappointment I just couldn't do it. He was convinced that he had talent as a songwriter and spent countless hours at home with his guitar, writing music. For years we would scrape together any money we had so that he could record his songs, none of which ever sold. This pattern continued for the entire duration of our eleven-year marriage.

When Aura was old enough to enter pre-school, I had a vision of opening a women's clothing boutique on the plaza in Sonoma. Michael's father, Mike, owned an insurance agency in Manhattan that primarily insured clothing manufacturers, many of them well known designers and top names in the business. With my previous outside sales experience I thought that we could make a go of it in a tourist town like Sonoma. We consulted with Mike and I researched various lines of clothing and accessories and also local real estate that might be available for lease. We went to the small business administration to see about the possibility of getting a loan and then by some miracle, a friend in a local bank offered us a small business loan to get started. It was risky, but we were aspiring and fearless. I leased a tiny retail space, upstairs in a recently remodeled Victorian House right off of the plaza. The building was lovely and would ultimately house a bookstore in the front, Peterberry's Café — Sonoma's first espresso café and still a legend today — occupying the center section and a gift shop doomed to failure in the rear. The upstairs housed Barclays of Sonoma and a Swiss Shop. This was an exciting enterprise for our young and hopeful family in 1976. The Victorian Court Bookstore was an intimate and cozy place. A visitor could come in to pick up a book, sit down to read with hot coffee and a warm beignet and browse through our little shops. I had visited open concept shopping spaces like this in Mill Valley in Marin and in LA and I thought that this retail concept had merit. Part of the image I had formed for our store included stocking the *Danskin©* line of exercise wear. Jane Fonda was the hottest thing in home exercise and a fitness franchise company called *Jazzercise* — which made exercise fun — had swept the nation, offering classes in every city. This was the precursor to all aerobics classes. Women wanted to look good in their exercise gear and I wanted to offer it to them in Sonoma. Chic clothing lines manufactured in India were also very hot, producing jewel-toned, 100% cotton skirts, blouses and pants at affordable prices. Women wanted unique sets of combs and barrettes for their long, beautiful hair and I sleuthed out a fabulous line from France and filled my little display case with these very feminine delights. On one of our trips back east to visit Michael's family, we were shopping in NYC and stopped in at the famous old *Kiehl's Pharmacy*. I was very taken by the selection of their natural-ingredient-based line of cosmetics and scented oils, many of which I still use. Their famous musk oil continues to be my scent of choice. When Barclays opened I had the full line of scented oils in their little brown bottles, sitting on top of my display case in a glass pyramid. Soon we had outgrown the tiny, upstairs space and when the gift shop folded, we moved downstairs adjacent to the café. The public loved the easy flow between the bookstore, café and our boutique. I was working six days a week, barely scratching out the dough to pay a part-time employee, but loving every minute. Handily enough, a Montessori pre-school had opened up in a church, directly behind our building. I enrolled little Aura, a very social child who was thrilled that she would be going to school. I was able to drop her off before I opened the shop, leaving a "back in 5 minutes" note on the door. Later she would play safely in and around the shops. Everyone knew and loved Aura. She had friends up and down East Napa Street and I never worried about her safety. After school, Curtis the friendly, singing barista who owned Peterberry's, would sit her down in the café, serving her cocoa with a warm, buttered brioche. We were not getting rich but we were happy.

The old Sonoma Greyhound Bus Depot had gone out of business. It had been prominently located on the northwest corner of the Sonoma Plaza, next door to the Christian Science Reading room and catty-corner to both the Sonoma Hotel and the El Dorado Hotel, since Greyhound had begun to run busses. This filthy spot was truly the armpit of Sonoma, in a great location. The Sebastiani family owned the entire corner, with its upstairs apartments overlooking the plaza. We had been checking out various prospective locations, hoping to find something directly on the square and this was it — a dump, but with potential. August Sebastiani was the landlord and I made a deal with him. He would allow us to spend a certain amount to fix up his building, which would then be pro-rated from the monthly lease payment. We shook on it and I hired a local contractor to come in and begin to gut the old building. The bus depot had been located on that corner for a good many years and I'm guessing that in all of those years it had not been cleaned even once. The walls literally ran with streaks of greasy, disgusting residue from all of the years of indoor cigarette and cigar smoking — and it stunk. We won't even discuss the condition of the bathroom. Yuck! The floors were ancient, cracked terra cotta tiles, but the building had graceful, arched windows and doorways. A very large arched doorway on the east wall still connects to a smaller space with an arched entrance on that side facing the street. The busses would pull in through that archway and slide open the giant door in the middle, allowing the passengers from the bus to pile out into the bus depot. We affixed that door closed, restored the plumbing and electrical and industrially cleaned the disgusting walls. Then the new, clean space was painted in neutral colors, dressing rooms, track lighting and new carpeting were added. It also had a spacious back room where we put a refrigerator, an old couch and area rug, creating a combination playroom, office and storeroom where Aura and her friends could hang out after school. The rent was astronomical for 1978, but we were convinced that in this prominent new location we would do business. During the same week that our grand opening was scheduled, we had some inclement weather and the entire shop was submerged under many inches of water. Our contractors came and pumped it out, sandbagging the rear. August had forgotten to tell us that the building was subject to flooding.

With the first emergency under our belts, opening day was scheduled. We had gone both to NYC and San Francisco to buy for the store. From NY, I was able to bring items not yet seen in our area like *LeSportsac©* bags, designer wear and color-tinted pantyhose, as yet unheard of in Northern CA. We had chic hats, upscale handbags, French espadrilles and little brightly colored, Chinese cotton Mary Janes. It was a fashion-forward boutique, and in retrospect, maybe a bit ahead of its time. Sonoma, however, was still the same sleepy little town. On any weekend you could drop a bomb in front of the store and not hit a car. Today, those same parking spaces are packed full of cars, bringing tourists to the wine country 24/7. But then it was tough going, financially juggling day by day. We hung in there in the new location for the next year and then I began to get the wine bug, and a yen to go back to school for wine-industry studies. At that time, Fresno State, UC Davis and Santa Rosa JC were the leading schools in our area offering wine industry-related course work. I was disheartened in the knowledge that I would have to close the struggling shop, yet the thought of going back to school and learning new skills was very exciting and gave me hope for the future. We must have been the first business people to sell a lease in town, as the *Sonoma Index Tribune* published the headline, Barclays Sell Lease. When the lease was finally sold to a chocolate-maker from the Napa Valley, we were completely broke, with invoices owing to various clothing manufacturers. Michael's father advised us to file for bankruptcy, but I stubbornly opposed this idea. Michael was still teaching and playing music, not bringing in much to help support us. Then I landed a job in a large women's clothing store in Santa Rosa and for the next year worked long hours while also going to school at night — eventually paying off every dime of the store's debts.

Given a choice I would gladly have become a full-time student, as going to school rang all of my bells. I loved every bit of it; taking courses in viticulture, enology, and wine marketing. When the day came that I believed I could walk into a winery, qualified to apply for a job, I set off on my job search. We lived within minutes of tiny, bucolic, Kenwood which was at that time home to five wineries; Kunde, Kenwood, Chateau St Jean, Landmark and St. Francis, all family owned and operated. As fate would have it, the very first winery I visited that day happened to be St. Francis Winery. Penny, or Ma Pen as everyone called her, hired me that very day to work weekends in the tasting room. My new job included vacuuming, dusting, cleaning the bathrooms and pouring wine for tourists. Soon enough I was working five days a week. The tasting room was a cozy, inviting space. A fireplace in the small gift shop was always blazing in the cooler months and there was a nice kitchen, with a beautiful patio in the back for parties. It felt like home. The winery was located in an unbelievably picturesque setting. Surrounded on all four sides by acres of green grapevines, it faced majestic Sugarloaf Ridge, which had a sprinkling of powdered sugar snow on top every winter. The art of retail sales came naturally to me. It was easy to promote the wines because in truth, they were just wonderful. I enjoyed chatting with the tourists who came from all over the world to taste Sonoma Valley wines. With Aura now old enough to ride the school bus, everything was perfect. I had a happy marriage, a bright, darling daughter and a great job. Surely it couldn't get any better than this.

After contentedly working at the winery for a few months and becoming very familiar with the wines, I decided to submit my resume for the possibility of outside sales work. Not yet having much of an opportunity to get to know the owner, Joe Martin, I worked up my courage to pay him a visit at his office. A small outbuilding across the parking lot from the tasting room, housed both the small office and a tiny bottling line. Entering the door to the office, Mr. Martin presented quite an imposing figure, seated behind a large desk piled with paperwork. He was a handsome man, weighing easily two hundred and fifty pounds, with lots of dark wavy hair, wearing a Ben Davis work shirt and huge work boots. He welcomed me into the modest space, offering his big, gap-toothed smile. Reading over my resume he wasted little time in telling me, "We've got distributors in almost every state now, but no sales rep in Sonoma County. Would you like to give it a try and see how you like it?" I could not believe my luck! For a mother of a young child, the offer of a local sales position like this which would allow me to be at home after school seemed too good to be true. The quality of the wines spoke for themselves, and I could hardly wait to start promoting the winery. It was like shooting fish in a barrel. Every day I went out and without fail came back with orders. We had a very small staff including: Joe, Tom Mackey the winemaker, myself, the office staff, along with various cellar rats who helped Tom and the vineyard workers. The office staff was astounded with the influx of new accounts and sales pouring in. As the secretarial staff rushed to type up those invoices, the guys in the cellar scrambled to get the orders out for delivery. Mr. Martin was ecstatic. One day he called me into the office and made me a terrific offer. "You're selling the heck out of all the stores in Sonoma County, how about focusing on restaurants for a while? I'll give you a commission on every single wine you can place on a wine list." He didn't have to ask me twice. Soon my paycheck had doubled from all of my wine list commissions. It wasn't long before Mr. Martin — Joe — had given me a desk right behind his in the little office. The secretarial staff was then moved to the offices above the wine-making facility — with its cellar full of wine barrels, shiny stainless steel tanks and the tiny lab for Tom. I was promoted, given the title of sales manager and looked forward to coming to work every day. My life was on an upswing. Joe and I were very compatible in the workplace. We would spend hours brainstorming crazy new marketing ideas. Joe asked me to set up a photo shoot of bottles. He loved the results and we put out a resulting 4-color photo — which was used for advertising for many years — on an elegant stand-up case card, which really caught people's attention in grocery stores. We spent hours making shelf-talkers with inviting descriptors, to be taped beneath rows of bottles in grocery and liquor stores. Then I initiated the Guest Chef program. My idea was to offer wine tastings to notable California chefs, asking them to provide us with recipes to be paired with a St. Francis wine. Many chefs participated and gave us recipes. We had these printed on recipe-box-sized, tear-off pads and hung them on the shelves below the bottles in stores. These were a big hit with shoppers, who bought the wine, then went home and followed the recipe. Soon we began promoting dinners in the tasting room using the recipes. People loved it! At that point I was given free rein to run with any viable idea that would promote the wine. In addition to having the title of sales manager, I also became the public relations director. I wrote educational pamphlets on topics such as dry farming, created the promotional brochures, participated in labeling and foiling design, organized and gave winery tours and headed up the Guest Chef program. Then we put together a huge event that was broadcast live from our cellar, on the San Francisco based culinary-inspired radio talk show, hosted by Narsai David. I was much too busy to continue on with outside sales and was allowed to hire and oversee local salespeople. In today's world, each of those departments would be headed by a separate person with its own staff. The work experience I gained then was a priceless gift, simply because Joe trusted and believed in me

I cannot remember even one incident of having cross words with Joe or being reprimanded for any action. Joe and his wife Emma lived in the cute country cottage on the property, a few yards away from the office. Often, in the mornings, he would come storming into the office with smoke pouring out of his ears, infuriated. I never mentioned his black moods and he never elaborated. But always, within minutes he would again become his charming, charismatic self, laughing and coming up with wild new marketing schemes. One day, as I was sitting behind him working at my desk, the door opened and in came Alan Hemphill, who was at that time the CFO from Chateau St. Jean Winery right across the street on Hwy. 12. "OK Martin, what's your secret weapon? You're on every g...d... wine list in this county." Blithely smirking, Joe pointed back at me saying, "There she is and you can't have her."

Joe and Emma had moved from San Francisco, selling Joe's

furniture business, Modern House. They had purchased the old Kenwood Behler Ranch in 1971, moving into the original Behler home, which had been built by Lou Behler's parents in 1913. While Emma commuted to work in the city every day, the former mister-man-about-town who had dressed in crisply starched, monogrammed shirts and jeweled cufflinks became farmer Joe in work boots on his tractor readying the future vineyards for planting. The first St. Francis vineyards were planted with Chardonnay, Riesling, Gewurztraminer, Cabernet Sauvignon, Merlot and Pinot Noir. For a number of years Joe sold his grapes to wineries such as Matanzas Creek and Sonoma Cutrer and then decided he might as well build a winery and make his own wine "instead of hauling them all over hell and gone in the heat." Joe's hobby and good source of income — buying and restoring old sets of flats in the city — resulted in Joe having acquired numerous construction skills. He could build or repair anything and loved tinkering with old clocks. With the help of the original owner, Lou Behler, who had become a trusted friend, they built the little winery that currently houses St. Anne's Crossing. Lou and Joe had no formal education past high school, but each in his own right was a mechanical and engineering genius. Lou was an incredible inventor and Joe really missed the boat by not going to engineering school. Joe and Lou would put their heads together and brainstorm for hours on new ideas. If the two of them were personally unable to build something, they would call in an expert to finish it. Joe spared no expense and the winery turned out to be a little gem.

My longtime friend Ed DeFault tells the story of living in Kenwood in 1971 and befriending his neighbor, Joe Martin. Joe, he said, was a "huge guy, easily 285 lbs." In 1978, Ed was working at Chateau St. Jean as a cellar rat, watching Joe beginning to build his winemaking facility across the road. "These were the infancy days of winemaking in Kenwood." As Ed tells it: "One hot summer day in August 1979, I went across the road and asked Joe if he needed any help and he said sure, I could use it." When Ed asked Joe how many guys were on the crew, Joe said, "This is it, just me and you. There was a bunkhouse behind Joe's house in the vineyard, which usually housed six to eight vineyard workers at any one time. Joe and Lou Behler had been pretty much been going it alone on the new building project. There was no vineyard foreman. Joe's right-hand man in the vineyard, Salvador Osegura, who was just a kid, oversaw the other vineyard guys." Ed talks about working day and night, eighteen to twenty hour shifts to bring in the first harvest in 1979. "We were building, harvesting and making wine all at once, doing everything by the seat of our pants." A couple of other guys came on to help with the building. Lou Behler was always on site helping Joe and coming up with brilliant and unique ways to get things done. The physical facility was built in stages and pads were laid for stainless steel tanks. Brad Webb, from Hanzell was the consultant for installing the jacketed tanks. Andre Tchelistcheff, "the dean of American winemakers," was also known to show up and offer consulting advice. Joe loved to tell his favorite story about Andre. The two of them were in the cellar, tasting the 1980 pinot noir. According to Ed, "The 1979 pinot noir was a total failure and the entire lot was thrown out onto the vineyard." When Andre tasted the wine, Joe recalled that Andre went down on one knee placing his palms together around the glass saying, "I beg you, pray, remove this wine from the barrel immediately!"

The new winery had a bond to make wine, but had no one with formal winemaking skills. Ed says that in 1979 he was the "de facto winemaker." Then Mike Richmond and Larry Brooks, from Acacia Winery brought in Chardonnay and Pinot Noir fruit to make their own wine and became Ed's mentors. "They were my teachers when I was learning how to make wine." Acacia paid no rent, but traded for their consultation expertise. St. Francis was also making wine on contract for William Hill Winery. "They had about 20,000 gallons — which seemed like a lot to us then. We were caretaking their wine and getting it into barrels, at the same time we were building the barrel room." Once the winemaking facility was completed, the construction crew turned their attention to the other old Behler house on the property. It was gutted and became the new tasting room. This house had been built in 1939, when Lou married his sweetheart, Dorothy. Ed recalls most of the major construction being completed by the end of harvest 1980. "Joe had lots of pressures and everyday setbacks. He was 100% committed and I looked up to him." Continuing with his story, Ed told me, "In August, 1981, after one hundred and eighty straight days of doing it all, Joe suddenly asked me to work part-time in order to create hours for another worker. I left instantly in a huff." Apparently Joe later called Ed to ask for the "keys to my winery." Ed says that he "dropped them in the mail."

The early 1970s were a pivotal time in California winemaking history. In 1970, an energetic and hardworking young man from San Francisco named Mike Lee, drove to Kenwood with his brother-in-law John Sheela. They went to the old Pagani Winery on Highway 12, to spend a day in the sun picking grapes for their former teacher from Santa Clara U., John Pagani. Julius Pagani, the founder of the winery had passed away and left the property to his brother John, who was ready to sell it. According to Kaarin Lee; when Mike and John Sheela saw the winery "It was love at first sight." Partners Martin Lee Sr., Mike and his brother Marty and John Sheela bought it and re-named it Kenwood Winery. Mike felt that he had found his true calling, getting right to work and learning quickly.

In 1972, Kaarin came to the winery for a picnic with some friends. She says, "When the tasting room door opened and out came fantastic-looking Mike Lee, my heart went ding, ding, ding and I think that Mike's heart did the same." Kaarin moved in with Mike just before harvest and became one of the first woman cellar-workers in the valley. There were prunes growing in front, along with the Johannisberg Reisling vines and what Kaarin remembers as, "the Sonoma field-blend reds." On December 8, 1973 Mike and Kaarin were married in the tasting room and went on to raise their two daughters Britt and Katherine, in the little house. She says that she was "smitten" watching the beautiful, cyclical patterns of nature, nurturing the growing grapes and vines, making the wine and the bottling — "so much fun! And then we would go to Mary's Pizza." Kenwood, she related, was so sleepy and sweet then, you'd know every single person who would pass in their car. Their vineyard manager Chuy Ordaz stayed with them for forty-four years and is still working for Kaarin. At first they bottled only in half- and one-gallon jugs, making deliveries to San Francisco in their old "hippie" mail truck. Her first job at the winery — she is proud to say — was shoveling stems. After the trucks would unload, Kaarin would drive them back to the field and dump the stems into the Kunde's field for their cows, "who would eat them and get high." Then she was the press operator for ten years, which is how she got acquainted with her neighbor and grower hot-tempered Joe Martin, who would bring his grapes to be weighed on their scales. "The true romance of the wine industry," she says, "is getting your hands dirty, working twelve- to fourteen-hour-days, being so tired you can't see straight and then having someone tell you that the next load due in was stuck in Geyserville — but don't worry, he'll be here in about an hour, so you'd better turn the lights on."

I first met when Kaarin, her sister-in-law Liz Sheela and Kaarin's mother came in to shop in my boutique, Barclay's of Sonoma. Later, after I had joined St. Francis, I visited Kaarin at their winery. She said, "I loved you from day one."

Our vineyard manager at St. Francis was the young and very serious Dino Amantite, first cousin to Julius Pagani. Dino begins his story, telling me: Julius had purchased the Pagani Winery property at the corner of Warm Springs Road — now Kenwood Winery — in 1884, raising cattle and planting crops of cherries and other fruit, hay and wine grapes. Dino's parents, Richard and Norma, brought he and his two brothers, Silvio and Mario, to the Valley of the Moon when Dino was thirteen. They purchased the idyllic property which was nestled into a sheltering hillside, across the road from the Kunde family's Wildwood Ranch, placing the big wrought iron letter P — made by Dino's brother Silvio — on the barn where it still hangs today.

The Pagani Ranch is arguably the single most photographed location in the entire Valley of the Moon. In the fall after harvest, when the ancient head-pruned Pagani old vine zins have given up their precious fruit and explode into exaggerated shades of burgundy, flaming oranges and yellows, cars stop and line up daily along Highway 12. Plein-air artists set up their easels along the roadway hoping to capture a likeness of nature's brilliance on their canvas and tourists park for photo ops.

Young Dino spent his adolescent years out of doors in beautiful, pristine Kenwood, hunting, taking care of the vines and driving the tractor, which to this day is his very favorite thing. He began dating his future wife Kari when he was nineteen. They married when he was twenty-one and have happily lived and raised their two sons in the valley. Kari's family moved to the Valley of the Moon in 1969. The family lived at the top of Moon Mountain Rd. on the Martini Ranch, home of the now-iconic Monterosso Vineyards. "There was not much to do in the valley then," she recalls, "There was Kenwood Winery, Chateau St. Jean and down on Madrone Rd. was Harry and Rita Parducci's Valley of the Moon Winery. That was it. I would do absolutely anything to get a ride down off of the mountain to visit with other people."

Dino credits his extensive and intuitive knowledge and love of viticulture to his mentors: Lou Behler — "a big German man" — Val Rossi, Enrico Gallo, his Uncle Louie Pagani and, Jim Sazzone "an old-fashioned Italian," the caretaker of Joe Martin's vineyards. "The knowledge I gained from the old-timers was and still is invaluable. They taught me how to learn about timing from nature." Dino remembers meeting his neighbor Joe Martin, who was driving his tractor between the Chardonnay vines in front of his house on Highway 12. "I introduced myself to this very big man with very big boots." Joe became a friend and mentor to Dino. In 1976 they took viticulture classes together from Rich Thomas at Santa Rosa JC, along with their neighbor Bill Kunde. In 1988 Joe asked Dino to take over the vineyard operations at St. Francis, offering him sole control — with respect to Dino's "one condition" — he had to be allowed to make time to take care of his family's ranch and vines — then and now — his main priority. Joe, he says was always respectful of this condition. Dino says that he learned to "go somewhere else" when Joe was unhappy. "He would get beet-red in the face, and you just knew. He loved to stir people up and was a terrible tease." Dino would give instructions to his vineyard crew and then Joe would come out behind him and order them to do just the opposite thing. Nobody argued with the big patrón. When Dino was hired on as vineyard foreman, one of the most important things he remembers doing, was re-grafting the vines, saying that he still takes great pride in "turning the Behler Ranch around" and helping bring the vineyards to their current prime condition. He also remembers getting along just fine with Lloyd Canton — Joe's business partner — "a good man." Apparently Joe "always had to have a project going on" and would start new projects without consulting anyone else, ignoring the winery budget. Lloyd would send Dino out looking for Joe to find out "What's Joe up to now? "But it was all good. I spent my youth there helping and learning. Joe was the founder of St. Francis. He put his life and soul into the place." Dino continued working as the vineyard foreman — "creating lasting relationships with our growers" — until the end of harvest 2008.

Tom Mackey and I had been hired on at the fledgling St. Francis at roughly the same time in the early 1980s. Another spunky Irish Catholic like Joe, Tom was bright, articulate and very serious about his winemaking. Tom says that he hit it off with Joe because he was just "so down to earth, but he was one serious prankster." At the time of Tom's hiring, Joe told him "We can't pay you a lot, but you would have complete control in the cellar." Tom liked that and says, "Joe, a natural salesman, had that big booming voice and would use it to really get things done." His goal, Tom says, was to "elevate the property." Originally there were along with Tom, a total crew of three guys. "Things were constantly breaking — hydraulics and electrical things — and Joe would just go in and fix them." One day, Joe fell off of the top of tank #11, breaking his elbow and then proceeded to drive himself, with one hand, to the ER.

The early case goods production stood at approximately 10-12,000 cases. To boost income, other brands such as Matanzas Creek, Acacia, Van der Kamp, Helen Turley and Sonoma Cutrer were alternately sharing the cellar. Joe had originally planted the varietal, Merlot, to be used as a blending wine. Planted and used for centuries, Merlot had traditionally been used to create world-famous, French Bordeaux blends. But it was not yet generally considered, in the U.S. wine world, to be a serious, stand-alone varietal. Tom had other ideas about that. St. Francis had begun producing and bottling 100% Merlot and I was advised to promote it as a wine which did not require years of time in the cellar prior to consumption. Joe called it his,"...Monday through Friday... wine. It's ready to drink right now, why wait?" This venerable old varietal began winning awards and selling like hotcakes at St Francis. People were beginning to pay attention to St. Francis Winery and it's winemaker Tom Mackey and we had to hire more staff to keep up with the demand. When I asked Tom why he thought this was, he said, "I think that it was the newness and small size of the winery — we were the new kids on the block — and of course, scarcity drives demand." At this time most good dinner houses were still having their menus printed and bound. If we ran out of the wine, they would have to have their menus reprinted at considerable expense and we would likely lose the account. The wines were selling so rapidly that the entire production went into an allocation process. We were obligated to make serious promises to our purveyors, that a certain number of cases would be held strictly for their use. This was very sticky. Once we made a commitment to a customer, ethically we had to stand behind it. A tug-of-war between Tom Mackey and myself developed and Joe too was not above making promises he couldn't keep. This became an uncomfortable point of contention, as each of us would make promises, taking from Peter to pay Paul, with one or the other of us looking badly in the end, but we always worked it out.

After the Koff Foundation purchased the winery, building at the new location on Pythian Road, the case production had risen to 300,000 cases. Tom remained with St. Francis until the end of the year, 2011. Today, Tom and his business partner Clyde Galantine have their own label, Tom Mackey Cellars.

Joe had purchased a case of small children's chalkboards and boxes of chalk for me to give away at restaurants and bars. He wanted me to sell wine by the glass. The concept, as yet unheard of in our area, was to convince the bartender or restaurateur, to offer a selection of wines to be poured by the glass. A standard sized 750ML bottle of wine will pour four glasses. If I could convince a bartender that it would be easy to sell off four glasses within an evening at the bar, everyone would make more money on the wine. At first the buyers would whine, "We'll be stuck with open bottles and have to throw out the rest." When I came back to the winery with that first order from the old Steamer Gold Landing in Petaluma — who agreed to try out our program — Joe was elated! Needless to say, this marketing concept was a no-brainer and caught on very quickly. My commissions skyrocketed.

Joe had a silent partner named Lloyd Canton who lived and worked in the East Bay. On the weekends he came to the winery to meet with Joe for grueling sessions of number crunching. I worked weekdays and for a long time was not aware of Lloyd's involvement with the winery. Then one day I was hearing chatter around the winery that Lloyd would be coming that day and everyone should look sharp. Joe was all fired up and angry and I clearly got the message that he was not looking forward to Lloyd's impending visit. Subsequent visits from Lloyd always seemed to elicit this same response and I would need to leave the office to get away from their heated discussions. I never inquired into Joe's personal business, but was in such close proximity that I could not help but hear many of their conversations. Joe always wanted to make improvements and start new projects and in response, Lloyd would be telling him to put on the brakes and stop spending. Lloyd was always polite to me, but during the early years he and Joe were like oil and water.

Five years down the road after I had first stopped in at St. Francis, things were going really well, both for our little family and for the expanding winery. Then a bombshell was dropped on my life. Seven years prior, Michael and I had been house-sitting for my friend David, high in the hills above the Sonoma Valley. One night a weird thing happened and the recollection is still clear as a bell. I was in the kitchen starting dinner and unwrapped a package of fresh trout that I was planning to prepare. When I opened the paper packaging and smelled the perfectly fresh trout, I had an experience that is difficult to describe. Immediately running for the bathroom I simulta-neously vomited, urinated and lost control of my bowels. At the same time, my entire body went into a very intense series of convulsions that threw me around the room, uncontrollably slamming me against walls, until I finally landed on the cold tile floor. It was a hideous experience and one I would not wish on my worst enemy. Michael watched helplessly, witnessing the entire scene. He helped to clean me up after it was over, and drove us home, but did not suggest that we go to a hospital. The next morning I drove myself to the local hospital where they immediately admitted me and proceeded to run tests for twenty-four hours. A doctor, who I did not know, came into my room and told me, "You are an epileptic, but I am not going to report this. Don't tell anyone or they will take away your driver's license." That was it. I was not prescribed any medication or scheduled for a follow-up appointment with a doctor. I got up, got dressed, left for work and opened the store. One evening, seven years later, again we were at David's house. He was now married with twin boys. I was working at a clothing store at a mall in Santa Rosa during the day and going to school at night. Each day after school, Aura would walk to David's house and I would come to collect her every evening. This pattern continued long after the time that I had begun to work at the winery. David and his wife Kari had moved to a lovely craftsman-style home, located close to Aura's grammar school. We were all watching TV after dinner when it happened again, only on a less dramatic scale. As my daughter now relates the story: suddenly my eyes rolled back into my head and I became unresponsive. Apparently everyone was crowded around me, calling my name. I don't have any memory of this. But what I do remember is Kari pulling me up and taking me outside on their porch "...to get some fresh air." Again, no one suggested that I go to the hospital.

As usual, I went through the motions of my life, as a wife and mother and going to work at the winery every day. But this time I had made an appointment with my doctor for a checkup. He scheduled me for a new type of test called a cat scan. At that time Sonoma Valley Hospital did not have a cat scanner, so I was scheduled at Memorial Hospital in Santa Rosa. The subsequent tests revealed that I had something called an acoustic neuroma. There was a sizable non-malignant tumor attached to my acoustic nerve — the eighth nerve — which had grown so large that it was not only pushing against and had begun to grow into my facial nerve — the seventh nerve — but was also pressing against my brain, causing what I was told were grand mal seizures. It was May 1986. I was thirty-eight years old and was scheduled for surgery at Memorial Hospital in Santa Rosa on mother's Day.

After five years of working closely with Joe, sharing that small office, we had become the best of friends. Pulling into the driveway of the winery, the morning after receiving the test results, I saw Joe walking toward our office. Opening the window to my orange Celica, I called out to him to come and get into the car with me. He was surprised but didn't question me and squeezed his sizable body into my little car. Not really having a plan or even knowing where I was going, I drove out onto Hwy 12 and turned on Adobe Canyon Road, which leads up to Sugarloaf Ridge State Park. Not far from the entrance to the park was the site of the shuttered Golden Bear Lodge, formerly a landmark restaurant situated in a dramatically picturesque, heavily forested setting. Turning into the parking lot of the deserted restaurant, I began to tell Joe about the brain tumor. It was a dramatic moment in my life when he burst into tears. We both cried as he gathered me in his ample embrace and rocked me like a baby.

In the pre-op conference, my neurological surgeon assured me that the medical services at Memorial would be excellent. He told us that the neuropathy unit had been recently upgraded and remodeled and assured us that he had performed numerous acoustic neuroma surgeries over the many years of his career. He did, however, inform me that it would be "likely" that I would lose the hearing in my left ear and a "possibility" that a "slight facial palsy" might occur. I discussed my concerns on the phone that night with my sister-in-law Justine, who lived in Maine. When I mentioned the possibility of facial palsy she said, "Oh no, that would never happen to you." I do not have any particular memories of sitting down with Michael and Aura to discuss this unpleasant development in our lives, as we did not want to frighten her. We went to the El Dorado for dinner the night before the surgery and I remember referring to it as "The Last Supper." I honestly did not expect to live through the surgery.

My mother had recently passed away, having fought a long and difficult battle with cancer. When I woke up in the ICU following my own surgery, my father was standing over me, patting and kissing me. My head and face were wrapped up like a mummy, the pain was intense and of course I was now legally deaf, having lost 100% of the hearing on my left side, due to the fact that the acoustic nerve had been removed in the surgery. I was in shock and very much surprised to find myself alive. I was told that my hair had been shaved from the left side of my head, in order to create a hole about the size of a fifty-cent piece — right behind my left ear — from which they had excised the tumor. I don't remember being in the hospital for more than a day or two and was then sent home with a nurse. My nose was running uncontrollably. There were piles of damp tissues on the floor next to my bed. Puzzled, Michael collected some of this fluid and took it to a lab in Santa Rosa where it was determined to be spinal fluid. Then he called the surgeon and related his findings about the spinal fluid. The surgeon informed Michael that I had a spinal fluid leak, which occurred during the course of the surgery. The dura — the membrane surrounding the brain, which allows the spinal fluid to circulate — had been nicked in the process. He told us that I would need to come back immediately so that he could go in again and repair the tear, or else I would be subject to the effects of spinal meningitis.

Prior to the surgery I had discovered the existence of the Acoustic Neuroma Association, who were hosting a conference at a large hotel in San Francisco. We went to the city and attended the conference, listening to the stories of survivors and made the acquaintance of an audiologist from Santa Rosa who was an acoustic neuroma survivor. One entire side of his body was palsied due to the effects of his acoustic neuroma surgery and many of the attendees to the conference were people left with partially palsied faces due to the sensitivity of the seventh nerve. We returned home discouraged and depressed.

I had an appointment with my longtime Sonoma MD who had originally discovered as he said, "the glitch in the cat scan," to have the bandages removed. When he unwrapped the gauze and my palsied face was exposed I was horrified and said, "Gosh Mike, you've got a really ugly wife." My face was unrecognizable. One half remained as it was, while the other half appeared to have melted. The left side of my mouth hung down. My speech was slurred. When I tried to eat or drink, the food or liquid simply spilled out of the open left side of my mouth. My left eyeball was nearly hanging out of its socket, completely exposed and I was unable to close it. Many people don't realize that the tiny muscles under our eyes are responsible for holding our eyeballs in place. The left nostril had collapsed, making it difficult to breathe. One eyebrow was significantly higher than the other. It appeared as if I had a stroke, only much more severe. When I cried, tears came only out of my right eye, which really pissed me off. For the next year I kept the eyeball lubricated and the eyelid taped shut with paper tape, which ripped out all of my eyelashes on that side. I was completely debilitated both physically and emotionally. So when we received the news about the spinal fluid leak, I declined the additional surgery unwilling to face the probability that in addition to my current state, my body might lose even more function. The surgeon was furious and in fact said to me, "If you won't allow me to perform the surgery to correct this problem, then I wash my hands of you! You'll contract spinal meningitis and die." At that moment, as often happens to people when faced with death, my spiritual side took over. I determined right then, if I did not rise from a supine position, logically, the spinal fluid could not flow out. So I lay flat on my back and visualized the tear in the dura healing. In retrospect, not one person other than the doctor who suggested to me that this was unwise or crazy, excepting for Michael — who was an avowed agnostic — questioned my motives. Instead, the phone next to my bed rang with callers inquiring, "How many drips today?" This went on for three full weeks, during which I was extremely careful to avoid a vertical position.

Michael would go off to the music store where he taught guitar lessons each day and I would fend for myself. Aura, who was now a very vulnerable twelve-year-old, did not seem to be too concerned about me and rarely offered to help me. In retrospect, I have wondered why we didn't do family counseling, but it was never discussed. Michael and Aura seemed oddly uncompassionate toward me. Conversely, scores of relatives, friends and neighbors came and went cleaning the house, bringing food and generally helping me in every possible way. Massage therapists and other body-workers volunteered to work on me. Finally, when I was able to answer the phone and say, "no drips today," I decided to remain supine for one additional week and visualize that leak completely healed, until I felt that it would be safe for me to rise and begin to resume my life. During this time my friend Joe Martin would come and sit by my bed, telling me jokes and cheering me up. He assured me that he wanted me to return to work as soon as I felt up to it. This was a ray of hope for me and I began to see some light at the end of the tunnel. My husband, however, complained about me "...getting fat," telling me, "I'd like to be with a woman who, when her ankles are touching, I can see between her thighs."

Feeling well enough to go back to work, I appeared in a large hat to cover my baldness and stitches, with my eye taped down, covered by large sunglasses. But nothing was ever to be the same. Most of my co-workers who had previously treated me in a respectful manner, now patted my arm and basically ignored me. Joe was overjoyed to have me back, but was probably hiding his horror at my new physical state. Things were going south at home too, but I was too traumatized to really see it. Then Michael left. There is no better way to say it. He just walked out taking almost nothing with him and never came back, giving me no explanation. I called his psychiatrist who told me, "I advised him to take a break. Don't worry, he'll be home in a few days." I was completely devastated and was incapable of stopping the flow of my tears. To this day I am still amazed that the human body has the capacity to continually produce the amount of liquid needed to support the rivers of tears, over which I seemingly had no control.

Aura had been taking gymnastics training at a gym in Petaluma for a few years. Prior to my illness we had a daily routine. Five days a week I would drive home from the winery, pulling up to the curb in front of our house where Aura would be waiting, with her snack and gym bag. Then we would take the forty-five-minute drive to Petaluma. Often I would go to the library and hang out before going back to collect her. Returning home I would prepare a full home-cooked meal for the three of us every night. After Michael moved out, he would pick up Aura and bring her home, dropping her at the curb. One night shortly after he had moved out, Aura came in carrying a long-stemmed, red rose. Stupidly, I assumed that he had sent it for me — but no — he had bought it for twelve-year-old Aura. She thought it was cool and couldn't understand why I would be upset. In fact, she couldn't understand why his moving out had distressed me. She told me, "Dad says that he just doesn't love you anymore" and apparently that was good enough for her. Before she graduated from middle school, Aura told me that she wanted to spend her summer at the Karolyi gymnastics camp in Texas. Bela Karolyi had come into the public eye, having been the famous gymnastics coach for tiny Mary Lou Retton. We watched Mary Lou win a gold medal, following her thrilling performance during the 1984 Olympics. In 1986, Bela and his wife Marta were living and working at their gymnastics camp in Texas. Having been out of work for some time and with little money forthcoming from Michael, I was dead broke. I was worried about Aura and wanted to be sure that she had a great summer. So I humbled myself and appealed to every single person I knew, to raise the money to send my daughter to camp. Undoubtedly, many of the people I approached felt sorry for us. I was able to raise the money in what today would be the equivalent of a Go Fund Me appeal, but then it was simply begging.

Things were not going well for me at the winery. In addition to my pathetic, debilitated physical condition and my extreme distress at having been abandoned by my husband at a time when I really needed his reassurance that I would recover, I was constantly on edge. Throughout our marriage I had believed in and supported Michael's artistic dreams and had always contributed my entire earnings to our joint checking account. In addition, I had been helping him to obtain an advanced degree. I was having trouble grasping the reality of my new situation. Within weeks after returning from the Karolyi's camp in Texas, I noticed that Aura's attitude toward me had changed dramatically. She returned as a rude and belligerent adolescent and blamed me for Michael having left our home and family, using my illness as the reason. Both my husband and my daughter blamed me and made me feel ashamed for my illness. Then Aura ran away. The sheer magnitude of personal loss, disregard, heartbreak, and betrayal was completely overwhelming.

Disillusion

Throughout her life Aura had always been an easy-going, cheerful child. An only child, like me, my little daughter was always content to entertain herself. If I gave her some art materials and a roll of tape, she would keep herself busy for hours. Her little record player was her favorite thing and she would sing along with her children's records. Always a big reader myself, I read to her and then she too became a voracious reader. She'd always had lots of friends and either was having sleepovers at our house, or was packing up her sleeping bag and going to sleep at a friend's house. In her elementary school years, I was the Brownie Scout Leader of a troop of twenty-three girls for three years and was always involved at the school and with the other parents. In her eighth-grade middle-school yearbook, Aura was listed as the "nicest girl in school," "best athlete," "sweetheart of the school" and she also received a mention for academics. Her gymnastic workouts at the gym in Petaluma had become so important to her that if she were ill, she would fake wellness in order to go to training. The gymnastic medals she had won at meets, hung from red, white and blue ribbons on the wall in her room and the local newspaper ran a full-page story about her.

As Aura tells me now, "I was already smoking pot in middle school" — and why not? We always had it in the house, where it was easy enough for her to access. Foolishly, it never occurred to me that she would do as we did. Parents can be blind to the bad behavior of their kids and will often say, "My kid is hanging out in a bad crowd," when, in fact, it could well be that their kid *is* the bad crowd. I don't know and don't want to know the circumstances that led up to Aura's big crash, but it was pretty scary being the parent having the experience. One morning at dawn I heard her footsteps in the hallway outside of my bedroom door. When I got up to check on her she was going out of the front door with a backpack full of clothes. Questioning her simply enraged her. She told me that she was leaving and had already made arrangements for a place to stay declining to reveal where this might be or how she would get there. Our argument grew heated and as she attempted to rush out of the front door I grabbed a handful of her long auburn hair, dragging her back in the direction of her room. Having never been treated like this before, she flipped out and ran hysterically out of the house. Later, I would have an epiphany; you can't tie up your kids and hold them hostage if they are determined to leave. Now I was the spectator, watching the most sacred threads of my life unravel and blow away in the wind like the fluff on a puffball from the garden, finding myself helpless against the all-encompassing negative circumstances of my life and the resulting unbearable pain from which there was no escape.

Aside from my boss Joe Martin, who seemed glad to have me back working at the winery and was always kind and supportive, my co-workers, on the other hand, seemed almost smug watching my emotional and physical disintegration. Where before I was the golden girl, now I was simply someone to be ignored and demeaned. Finally, it became clear to me that I could not fulfill the obligations of the public relations director with a bald head, a severely paralyzed face and one eye taped down, prone to tears at any given moment. I discussed this with Joe and gave my notice, but before giving up my job, I trained another capable woman to take my place in sales and pre-sold every single bottle of the upcoming vintage leaving St. Francis Winery in a very enviable position.

My life was shit. Completely alone, I was receiving a small allotment of unemployment disability insurance from the winery and $200 per month child support from Michael, not enough to pay my modest mortgage or the utilities. I had nothing and had lost everything, my nuclear family, my persona and physical resilience and my career, all of my reasons for living. Paying a visit to the local sheriff's office and tearfully relating my story, the officer at the desk was quite clear with me: "Mrs. Barclay, the state of California has no laws governing runaway minors and will provide no assistance in their return." The officer went on to explain that in the state of New York there was a law called, *Alienation of the affection of minors.*" To explain this most simply, let's say that in most cases an angry teenager runs away and goes to a friend's house. In a normal, well-adjusted home a responsible and compassionate parent of the household would call you to say that your angry child was there and safe so that you would not be worried. They might keep the child for the weekend and then return them home. But it was not unusual for some adults to consider themselves a better buddy to your child, than an actual parent. In this case, the buddy adult will keep your child without informing you, actually thinking that they are doing the child a favor by going along with their adolescent belief system. In the state of New York this is against the law, but not in California." The officer then proceeded to procure a law text and read me the actual statute. But it was the last thing that he said to me that blew my mind; "Mrs. Barclay, for your sake, I sincerely hope that your daughter does not break any major laws. For instance, if she were under age eighteen and fire-bombed a school you would be held completely responsible for all damages and would likely lose your home. Good Luck!"

Michael rented an apartment in Sonoma and Aura went to live with him. Totally unsupervised there — Michael would leave early in the day and not return back until the evening — Aura was allowed to live completely out of control. On one occasion when I visited her at the apartment, she introduced me to her "boyfriend," obviously an adult man. She said to me, "...this is our place and we can do whatever we want here." Michael supported this behavior in his fourteen-year-old daughter. Both Michael and Bill — who had become a full-time alcoholic — kept Aura and made arrangements for her to stay at various households until, progressively, each discovered that she was unmanageable and asked her to leave. She was not going to school. A mother in one of the households actually had the nerve to call me, lecturing me about what a bad mother my daughter claimed me to be and demanding that I turn over my pitiful $200 child support to her. I responded by telling her that every single morning my phone would ring with a call from the high school, informing me that my daughter was truant. My request to her was, if she would go to the school and sign the responsibility card so that the calls would then go to her phone instead of mine, I would gladly relinquish the $200 per month to her. She, unwilling to take the responsibility, refused. Aura moved from household to household for two years. Neither of her fathers would provide me with an address or phone number to reach my child and I had no money for an attorney. One day I received a call from the Sonoma police station to say that they were holding my minor child. I now forget why they were holding her, but guess that it must have been for something minor like shoplifting or truancy because she had not been charged with a crime. I went to retrieve my daughter as the law required. After signing her out, we stepped outside on to the curb and she said to me, "Thanks for nothing. F--k you bitch," and walked off. I had no legal right to detain her. So I sat down on the curb in front of the police station and cried.

During the course of those missing years, many events happened in my life. First, I decided that I had nothing to live for and made specific plans for my suicide. I had a number of close friends who were nurses and figured that between them I would be able to procure enough sleeping pills to kill myself. Always a serious walker/hiker I walked for hours every day high into the wilds of Sonoma Mountain. Finally, I determined that I would hike for a few hours up into a secluded, wooded place, lie down under a tree and take the pills. Hey — no muss, no fuss, no cleanup. I would let the vultures take me in the Tibetan manner and just be gone. No biggie. But later my rational mind kicked in and said, "Either shit or get off the pot." So instead this is what I did: I joined Al-Anon, which forever changed my life, found a meditation group and began to participate on a regular basis and went for therapy. Each of the various therapists that I consulted over the course of those years told me exactly the same thing in so many words; that I had "...undergone the kind of physical and emotional shock that would likely make the average person want to give up on life" and that I was to be "...commended for taking the higher road instead." None of this offered a substitute for actual happiness, but did provide a foundation for creating a future peace for me. At one of my therapy sessions I also had the realization that for the entire duration of my eleven-year marriage to Michael I had not been on a horse or created any art. I had given over my entire passion for art into his musical aspirations. What a shocker. It was then that I knew that I had better get back on track with my true self.

Insight
Into Recovery

During my first, very solitary year of emotional healing at home, I embarked on a course to satisfy one of my longtime ambitions. When I was nineteen, I read a nutrition textbook that someone had given to me. Among myriad other things, it described the process of digestion in the human body in detail. My mother had been a very good cook and would allow me to come into the kitchen to try out new recipes. Eventually, I developed a passion for food and cooking. During my high school years I hosted dinner parties, preparing all of the dishes myself. My home economics teacher was so proud. These menus for my dinner parties went way beyond the snickerdoodle cookies we baked in class. My father, who owned a business in San Francisco, would bring home entire sides of beef, lamb, and pork, which had been cut, dressed, and deposited into our home freezer for future dinners. Having been raised on beef filets and now reading how long it took for that meat to leave our bodies and what happened in between, did not make me happy. I went cold turkey on red meat and have never had another hamburger since. A true vegetarian for quite a number of years and throughout my pregnancy with Aura, I eventually embraced a Mediterranean style diet that included lots of fruits and vegetables, fish and poultry. My history as a lifetime vegetable gardener has usefully provided me with a good foundation for an interest in good food and a healthy lifestyle.

Since those teen years, when I read the nutrition text, I

harbored a desire to become a nutritionist. My goal was not to be a dietician and work in a hospital setting, but rather to study biochemistry and open my own private practice, which I eventually did. I enrolled in a distance-learning, nutrition school. I was an early MAC user and had my first little Apple computer, compliments of my father (God Bless Him) who had come to my financial rescue, "Until you are able to get back on your feet." I lived on a quiet street in Glen Ellen and was able to study and work without distraction. After two years I graduated from The University of the State of New York Education Dept., Office of the Professions, receiving both a license number and certificate number registering me to work as a Certified Dietitian-Nutri-tionist.

A meditation group met weekly in Sonoma, in the tiny home of a wonderful lady named Marge, who had been hosting a setting for Vipassana meditation for years. One of my therapists recommended that I try out this group. Right away I knew that it was a perfect fit for me. I kept going back each week. One of the people who attended this group was a tall, slender, silver-haired man with piercing blue eyes and very chiseled cheekbones — Dr. William Stablein. William had earned two PhDs, one in psychology and another in philosophy. Many years earlier he had gone to India with his wife, on a Fulbright scholarship, to study Tibetan Buddhism. They stayed for five years. William had been a highly respected psychologist and scholar in the Seattle area and his wife was a published poet of some renown. William was writing a book entitled *The Great Black One* (the Mahakala). This book was the product of his years of life and study in the traditions and practices of Mahayana and Vajrayana Buddhism. William and his teenage daughter had come together to Sonoma, living in a country home belonging to his mother-in-law. It wasn't long before William asked me out. Frankly, I was shocked and surprised, due to the appearance of my face. Where before I was a man magnet, now men no longer gave me a second look. My face, however, did not seem to be a factor in William's attraction to me and we soon became a serious couple, engaged in what would become the most passionate and significant love affair of my life. Eventually, William moved in with me. It is said that the universe will bring exactly what one needs and in this case, William's total adoration of me and support of my endeavors had a huge impact on my personal healing process. He supported my work and educational pursuits and I helped him in the editing process for his book. In addition to his psychology practice, he taught classes in Tai Chi and offered classes in Sanskrit.

Following a year of rest and recovery, I began again looking for work at wineries. My resume, a portfolio containing samples of much of my work from St. Francis, was quite impressive. Joe Martin provided glowing references. I went for second and third, great interviews at prestigious wineries in both Sonoma and Napa but they inevitably concluded in exactly the same manner. Always the final interviewing executive would ask, "What happened to your face?" These interviews — more than simply discouraging — were unbearable and depressing, as there was nothing that I could do to remedy this problem. My face was and continues to be the first thing that everyone sees and judges. No matter where I went, whether I was getting in or out of an elevator or paying for gas at the gas station, someone would ask me, "What's wrong with your face?" Too often they would also offer unsolicited solutions such as, "you should see my acupuncturist" or " I can recommend a great plastic surgeon." Children would, and still do, point and stare. It was becoming ever more difficult for me to be comfortable in public. My friend Barbara was working at The Beltane Ranch, a Bed and Breakfast in Glen Ellen and brought me along with her one day to meet the owner, Rosemary Wood. This was a very special place and Rosemary was a very special person. She hired me at minimum wage to help with just about everything at the b & b. I did laundry, changed sheets, cleaned bathrooms, worked in the garden and helped out in the kitchen, also serving breakfast to the guests. This was a giant career step-down from my previous executive position at the winery, but I felt safe and appreciated at Beltane and was grateful to have the job.

I joined a low-cost gym in Petaluma, in hopes of at least helping to restore a measure of well being to my body. During the acoustic neuroma removal surgery, the middle ear on the affected side had also been removed, leaving me balance challenged. I was determined to regain my physical dignity. Returning each day from the gym brought the welcome reward of a fine sense of physical pleasure, after working my body as hard as I could. Basically all I did was sleep, eat, work out and repeat the pattern. Soon my clothes and those horrid thong leotards we wore then, looked good on me and other clients at the gym began asking me to train them. Inquiring at Santa Rosa JC, I found that they offered many interesting classes, which would help me to obtain a fitness certification. I enrolled, taking additional nutrition, as well as sports physiology and anatomy classes. I also took a math course but I was unable to pass. My MD had diagnosed me citing residual effects of the surgery, as "disnumeric" and "aphasic." Surgery that interferes with the brain in any manner can have weird and far-reaching effects and in my case, had reduced my capacity for any type of mathematics back to an elementary level. This was yet another blow, as formerly I had been the numbers cruncher at St. Francis. So I also signed up for the head injury program. The aphasia was another thing entirely. I had always prided myself on having a reasonably good vocabulary. Now, words that had been familiar and second-hand were elusive to me. It took me minutes or longer to name familiar objects or describe much of anything at all, and still do to this day. I have to write down suggestion words to myself. Eventually, the word I have been seeking may surface. Neighborhoods that were completely familiar became challenging to navigate. At school, I had to work twice as hard as anyone else to get by. Nevertheless, I was making A's and getting pats on the back from my instructors. Later, when I began to test for various fitness certifications I had to study like crazy and in the end, received certifications through numerous organizations. My partner William was more than supportive throughout this period of time, helping me study for exams and building my self-esteem with his positive and open attitude.

My sweet and loving father passed away, leaving me our family home in Marin. Meanwhile, I was working as a Personal Fitness Trainer at the Parkpoint Club in Sonoma and was teaching water aerobics there as well. I was also teaching water aerobics at two senior communities in the Sonoma Area and began to be in demand to lead classes in private pools throughout the valley. Later, I was hired at the Sonoma Mission Inn as a Personal Fitness Trainer, teaching water aerobics there, giving private nutrition consultations and private aquatic therapy to their guests, while I also maintained an office in Sonoma offering nutrition consultation

One day in the locker room of the Parkpoint Club, I overheard a woman seeking help to exercise her horses. Introducing myself, I learned that she was Jan Keen, wife of the local author Sam Keen. They owned Peruvian Paso horses and needed help keeping them fit while Sam was on book tour. This was another pivotal moment for me, as Peruvian horses were to become a lifeline to my own recovery.

I had retained the health insurance from my marriage through my divorce, which would cover the expenses for some reconstructive surgery for my face. A technique had been developed whereby the surgeon would remove the *sural nerve* from the calf of one leg. Then, peeling back both sides of my face, would remove the non-functioning seventh nerve from the face and replace it with the fresh, living sural nerve. In the first phase of these surgeries, surgeons would open my face from the tip of one ear — exposing the seventh nerve — across the top of the upper lip and over to the other ear, removing the non-functioning section of the seventh nerve. Next, the fresh sural nerve from my calf would be transplanted and reconnected, in the hope that within six months it would be generating enough electricity to allow the return of facial reanimation. Following the nerve transplant, UCSF was my home for two weeks. During that time I didn't hear from my daughter. My cousins Marcia and Jim came to the hospital, bringing food and flowers and drove me back to Sonoma. My face was swollen up like a multi-colored balloon. When they released me from UCSF I went right back to the Parkpoint and humbly resumed training my private clients, bruising and all. Due to the removal of the leg nerve I was unable to walk without aid. So every day I crutched into the gym and worked the heck out of my upper body in an attempt to retain my strength. When the pain in my leg subsided enough that I felt that I could resume training on my lower body, I rehabbed myself.

Six months later I was scheduled for the second phase of the restoration process. A large section of the *serratus muscle* on my left upper torso, where the serratus originates under the armpit would be resected. Re-opening the left side of my face to expose the connection site of the previously implanted facial nerve, a section of my serratus muscle that had been harvested was implanted in my cheek and connected, leaving — yet another — large scar from underneath my arm and halfway down my side. This time I stayed at UCSF for three weeks. Again, my cousins, aunts, and uncles, provided support. Following this surgery, I was unable to use my upper body and so I dutifully went to the gym and worked my lower body ever more rigorously. My doctors told me that I would hopefully regain facial reanimation to the left side of my face within another six months. The holidays came and went showing no change. The entire process — pain, rehab, and hospital bills — was for naught as the surgeries had failed to restore any movement to my face. People at the various gyms had apparently been watching me though, and my practice as a trainer began to grow. My schedule was very full and finally I was able to stop worrying about making ends meet.

In the fall of 1989, I made the decision to move from the house where I had been living in Glen Ellen and look for a place that would accommodate horses. My relationship with William had amicably come to an end and I was ready to move on. Following an extensive search of the entire Sonoma Valley, area I found a property in foreclosure. It was a three-and-a-half-acre property in Glen Ellen situated on a year-round creek, with a spacious house, two large pasture areas for horses and an old sheep barn. The front door opened onto a large living room, with a fireplace and a picture window framed by a cushioned window seat with a magnificent, unobstructed view of Sonoma Mountain. A large formal dining room completed the opposite side of the entrance. A sliding pocket door revealed a large airy great room, an adequate kitchen with lots of storage, a bathroom and a laundry room. Large windows flooded the room with sunlight and provided a serene view of the upper acre of property. Sliding doors opened onto a patio in back. Down a hall were three bedrooms, one of which would become my jewelry workshop and a large master bath. The price on this house, due to the foreclosure, had been reduced tremendously and was now within my budget. With the funds from both the sale of my home and my family home in Marin, I was in a position to buy it almost outright. The two front rooms became my fitness studio and I lived in the remainder of the house. The former living room space became the gym, which I equipped with every single piece of equipment one would need in a fitness setting. In the former dining room, the walls were mirrored floor-to-ceiling and a barre was installed. This would be the Pilates studio. Everything was almost complete. The last step would be to find the perfect horse.

All along, I had been going up to the Keen's Sky Ranch, situated near the top of the Mayacamas mountain range between Napa and Sonoma, to help exercise their gorgeous Peruvian Paso horses. Sam's spirited pitch-black mare, Asia, was my favorite. Riding with Jan, her daughter Jessie and other friends up into the mountains surrounding their extensive ranch property, I was quickly becoming friendly with the Keen family. Sam called me at home one day and asked if I would like to take ownership of his horse? *Would I?* He appeared a few days later with his horse trailer and made me a gift of his beautiful Asia. I was rapturously over the moon. Now I had a charming little ranchette, a fine house, a thriving private practice and a horse grazing in my pasture. For me it didn't get much better than that. But still, my daughter was out on the streets. The worry kept me awake at night. The Al-Anon teachings reminded me that I was powerless to help.

Fleeting Moments
Of Peace

My new property was, ironically, located adjacent to a drug and alcohol rehabilitation center. The owners at the facility hired me to work with their recovering addicts in the pool in the summer and indoors in the winter. This was a convenient place for me to attend Al-Anon meetings. I also spent many months in their kitchen working as the cook. That year when I turned in a stack of 1099s, my tax guy could not believe his eyes when he saw how many hours I had worked at all of my various jobs.

Working at the rehab center was a real eye-opener for me. The Al-Anon concepts had become very important to me and quickly became healthy, useful tools, in the management of every facet of my life. They did, in fact, completely change my way of thinking about many things. Then, learning about the existence of Alateen — a program for teens, whose lives have been affected by someone else's drinking or drug abuse — I volunteered to become an Alateen sponsor. Working with the Alateens became more than meaningful for me. I was an Alateen sponsor steadily for seven years, mentoring various groups around Sonoma County. Because AA and Al-Anon are programs based on anonymity I am unable to elaborate further on these pages.

My friend Sharmaine had made me a gift of her gorgeous, registered Peruvian Paso stallion, Tejo de Oro — the gold coin — a golden palomino with a white mane and tail. I had loads of pasture space and turned him in with Asia, with the hope that they would breed. Tejo was a sweet and gentle stallion. He could be ridden bareback with only a halter and was always a perfect gentleman. This was a memorably peaceful time in my life. I remember sitting in the window seat and gazing out onto the grassy pasture, watching the lovely black mare with her golden stallion. This pair immediately became bonded pasture mates and appeared to be very contented in each other's company.

The gestation period for an equine is typically eleven months. About halfway into her pregnancy, my beautiful Asia began to lose weight and appear unwell. Dr. Pete came to examine her and we decided that he should give Asia an ultrasound, the first of many he would administer during this pregnancy. The tests always showed the foal to be alive, but the mare looked haggard and the vet said, "She is only staying alive to give you her baby." We were prepared for the worst. One spring morning in 2008, close to Asia's due date, I found her lying down alongside the creek. Tejo was standing over her, agitated and whinnying. Then I saw the sack present from the mare. Haltering Tejo, I quickly took him to the upper pasture. Running back down to the barn I could see the entire sack on the ground, with the foal presented hooves first. In a normal, healthy birth, those sharp, tiny hooves tear the sack open and the foal will wiggle out and stand up. But the foal was still and the sack unbroken. Using my fingernails I ripped open the sack between the little hooves and watched in amazement as my little foal took his first breaths and then wiggled out. Then I cut the cord and the little guy jumped right up. He fell over the side of the creek bed and began rolling down toward the swiftly running creek. At that moment, I was grateful for my strong body. Scooping him up and running for the barn, I gently placed him in the stall that had been prepared with fresh shavings in anticipation of the birth. Asia got up and followed him into the old barn. I had been guessing that I would get a little buckskin foal — a golden body with black points. But much to my surprise, here was a bright-red chestnut with four perfectly matching white socks, and a silver mane and tail like his dad. I named him Milagro de Oro — miracle of gold — having saved his life both from suffocation and almost drowning in the creek before he was even one hour old. Dr. Pete arrived right away and we decided that the baby should be given an extra dose of colostrum, a naturally occurring antibiotic usually present in the first mare's milk. Even though the mare was still alive and the foal was suckling we were could not be sure how much nutrition her milk would actually provide, given the current state of her health. The best possible mama, Asia kept the foal immaculate offering him every ounce of her energy and allowed the baby to nurse at will.

Knowing that she could not possibly have much milk to offer, even though the foal nursed regularly, I immediately began to supplement him with a 3:1 Foal Lac and goat's milk solution. The vet advised against bottle feeding — "You'll have a ball and chain." Milagro learned to drink from a small bucket right away. My former client, Laura Chanel the cheese-maker, had a goat farm. She offered me donations of goat's milk and advised me to pasteurize it myself before combining it with the Foal Lac/powdered milk solution. I was feeding on a 2-hour/24-hour schedule while continuing to work my full-time job. This continued for three continuous weeks, in order to keep the little guy alive. My refrigerator was chock full of foal solution in glass canning jars.

The baby was doing fine, but the mare was in a state of serious decline, with no positive diagnosis. She was suffering terribly and I had to make the painful decision to have her euthanized. When the dreaded day arrived and little Milagro was only three weeks old, Dr. Pete advised me to bring Tejo back down with Milagro to look after him, "He is such a gentle and sensible stallion...." This advice would normally be contrary to common horse husbandry practices, as stallions have been known to attack and kill foals. But the vet's intuition was right on the mark. Although I was grief-stricken at the loss of my beloved mare, it was very comforting to watch the good father and his tiny son thriving together. Over the course of the next year, Tejo was returned to Sharmaine and several babysitting mares were brought in to keep Milagro company.

I needed a new riding horse and began searching for another Peruvian Paso. Throughout the course of my life I had owned various Quarter Horses, Arabians, mixed breeds and Maggie, my Standardbred. But the smooth, magical gait of the Peruvian horses, their unusual beauty and fine dispositions had me hooked on this breed for life. There was a breeder and Peruvian Paso show judge named Mary who lived in Idaho. We had been emailing back and forth and she seemed to know exactly what I was seeking, a young Peruvian gelding with the sturdy conformation of a quarter horse. After searching for an entire year, Mary directed me to an older couple that lived in her vicinity. They were selling their ranch and stock. Their mare had been bred to Mary's awesome stallion El Tumi and she said that the offspring, a young gelding, was a beauty. Following a clean vet check on the horse, I agreed to purchase him and said that I would have a shipper bring him to California. The owners of the horse would not hear of it saying, "We won't sell him to just anyone, we'll trailer him down ourselves and inspect your place." So Clark and Neela made the trip to California from Idaho with their horse. Amigo was five years old and for the most part, untrained. When they backed him out of the trailer and I was able to get a good look at him, it caused me to catch my breath. This glossy black gelding stood at over fifteen hands, tall for a Peruvian Paso horse and full muscled. He had the most beautiful eyes I had ever seen on any horse. His wavy black mane flowed all the way down to his shoulders and his tail touched the ground. I insisted that Clark and Neela stay with me, instead of going to a motel. We spent a wonderful weekend together and remained very good friends for many years to come. They left with an empty horse trailer.

Amigo was pastured on the grassy acre above the house, while Milagro and his pasture mate Penguina stayed in the lower pasture. He was wild and crazy up on a hill by himself, refusing to allow me to get near him. It took considerable time and a lot of wet saddle blankets, but eventually Amigo ended up being the best trail horse I ever owned. Amigo and Milagro were, eventually, inseparable pasture mates for many years to come.

Finding myself booked solid with private training appointments I was forced to give up most of my other work and focus on my private practice at home. Each day would start with my first client arriving at 7AM. Although I was perennially sick with worry, concerned about the wellbeing of my daughter, every morning I would put on a big smile and answer the door. Seeing clients on the hour, I would stop at noon and drive to whatever aquatic class I was scheduled to teach that day, shower and drive home to meet my next client. Usually, I did not finish with the last client until 7PM. I had a fabulous, deep, year-round tan which has later come back to bite me in the manifestation of spotty, sun-damaged skin. For a few years I worked seven days a week, then tapered off and started taking the weekends for myself, using my free time to ride the unlimited, scenic trails in Sonoma County and horse camping at Pt. Reyes National Seashore in Marin.

Over the course of the twelve years in which I lived on that particular property, many private clients came to see me, some multiple times per week for training or rehab for injuries. Many of them remain close friends to this day. Page Masson had made an appointment for training. At first glance Page appeared to be a diminutive, silver-haired grandmotherly type. But as soon as she spoke her first words to me, I realized that indeed "a book should not be judged by its cover." This little lady was a pistol, telling me that her doctor had advised her to give up kickboxing classes and go for weight training, which would hopefully cause her fewer injuries. The two of us hit it off immediately and we became fast friends during the years that she trained in my studio, often multiple times per week. She and her husband Charlie had invited me to their home for dinner. Then, Page and I would meet for lunch when we could find the time. She was a relentless volunteer at various charities in the county, but was especially interested in advocating for animals and animal rights. In her spare time, Page would acquire carloads of clothing from the thrift store where she volunteered. She would take them home, often spending the entire day washing and folding the clean clothes. Then, parking alongside Highway 12, she would walk out into the vineyards where she could see workers toiling, giving them bags of clean clothes to take home for their families. That was who she was, a role model for me. Charlie had been raised near Davis on the historic Nut Tree property, a popular spot for travelers to stop, have lunch, ride the miniature train and spend pleasant hours with their families. Page and I were chatting one day when she casually mentioned the fortune that they had acquired when Charlie sold the Nut Tree. Looking at her, one would never guess that she had a cent, as she typically wore clothing from the thrift store. But I came to discover that they were notoriously philanthropic. One Monday morning during her session, Page asked me as usual, "How was your weekend?" Often I would relate my glorious weekend tales of horse camping in Pt. Reyes. She said,"… it seems like most of your friends have RVs to sleep in on these trips and you sleep in the shell of your pickup." She went on to tell me that she and Charlie had a good RV that they wanted to give to me as a gift. Imagine my delight when Charlie pulled into my driveway with a twenty-seven-foot Winnebago in pristine condition that slept six and had a kitchen and bathroom. This was way beyond my wildest cowgirl dreams. I had it fitted out with a brake controller to pull my horse trailer and had loads of fun equipping the kitchen and putting a feather bed on the spacious overhead double bed. Future weekends found me spending many heavenly nights at the National Seashore with my horses. In the years following my marriage to Joe Martin in 2004, I found no more time for camping and had little need for my cool Winnebago. At that time, a serious cowgirl friend, named Veda Rose and her boot-maker husband, RC had lost both their rental home in West Sonoma County and Veda's job, during the housing crash. In addition, RC was quite ill. Knowing that they had nowhere to go, I offered them the RV as a gift. Veda and I went to the DMV, transferring the title, paying it forward. They moved into the RV where they lived for years until RC passed away. Later, Page told me that I was "a good learner."

One day a new client named Nancy Ryan arrived at my fitness studio, requesting a workout plan. She had noticed my horses grazing in their pasture, on her way up the driveway and was curious to know what breed they were? As I got to know her, she told me about the horse farm at Sonoma Developmental Center, where she boarded her horse Fudge. SDC was only minutes from my place in Glen Ellen and was adjacent to Sonoma Valley Regional Park, with great trails for riding. Later I would join the Regional Parks Mounted Assistance Unit, the State Parks MAU and also the SDC Mounted Posse, which all required a rider to log monthly hours in order to remain a member. For many years to come I would load a horse — first Penguina, the adorable little black and white paint Peruvian mare, borrowed from my friend (the late) Judy Collins after losing Asia — into the trailer and drive to the park to ride. Often, I would meet up with Nancy R to spend quiet hours on the trail. She was a schoolteacher, who had married my old friend Richard Neiss the piano player and had two young sons. Both hailed from the East Coast. Nancy was very adventurous, always game for absolutely anything. She would go horse camping at the drop of a hat, tossing a can of tuna, a jar of peanut butter, a candy bar and a bottle of tequila into a sack and take off. Conversely, I would spend time the night before making up a batch of succulent kosher tuna and hardboiled egg with cucumber, the way my mother had made it, and added capers for good measure, home-baked bread, chocolate truffles and a bottle of good wine to share. But in other ways, we had a lot in common and would discuss movies, books, the state of the world and of course, horses. Amigo's owners had mailed me a homemade video. It showed him dancing around in an arena and also included some photos of his mother, a tall, pitch-black, registered Peruvian Paso mare. We had dinner at my house and watched the video, both of us were entranced with this feisty young gelding. Nancy was adamant. "You've got to have him!" The rest is history.

The two of us had been camping at the Stewart Ranch Horse Camp in Point Reyes for a few days. Out there on the vast, lush lands of the National Seashore, one could ride for days and never cross the same trail twice. The West Marin scenery is awe-inspiring and majestic; encompassing a variety of densely wooded, indescribably scenic terrain from mountaintops to the sea. In my saddlebags I always carried binoculars — handy for gazing up into the tops of gigantic redwoods to view an eagle's nest, or to spy on the agile, snow-white deer that populated this area. Other mandatory equipment included a headlamp, should we find ourselves still riding when night fell — treacherous! — a first aid kit in case of the inevitable injury, a package of Benadryl, in the event we unwittingly blundered into the ubiquitous stinging nettles that abounded in the Pt. Reyes forests, a multi-use knife and snacks. One warm and crystal clear morning, we arose and decided to make the all-day trip down to Wildcat Beach and back. It was hot and there was a pond where we could cool off and have our lunch on the way down. Maybe halfway down the trail, passing only a few other riders, we were astonished to see a saddled, riderless horse galloping furiously up the trail. Courageous young women, we jumped down from our own horses, arms akimbo in an attempt to block the trail and stop the poor, panting, sweating horse. We halted the pretty and very frightened mare in her tracks. She was fully tacked and oddly had a piece of string hanging from her halter. Obviously, some knucklehead had tied up this mare with a piece of twine. There was only one way up or down to the beach and so we continued down, ponying the runaway horse on a spare lead rope behind us, knowing that we would meet the owner coming up on foot. Sure enough, there came a small party of riders including a duded-up cowboy with feet on the ground, embarrassed as all get out. Later we joked about how easily we could have stolen that cute little mare.

Years later, when I had remarried and was living on my husband's fifty-five-acre ranch in Windsor, Nancy trailered her freckled white Arab, Woodrow — "Don't call him Woody, his name is Woodrow!" — up Hwy. 101 to ride with me. The ranch where I lived was surrounded by hundreds of acres of vineyards, which made for lovely riding in the soft soil. It was also just minutes away from Riverfront Regional Park, which as its name implied, was scenically situated along the banks of the Russian River, winding around a picture-perfect lake. The park rules and regulations required visitors to stay within the park boundaries. But almost every day, making my own rules, I cut through the park and rode alone for miles along the river, often not arriving back home until dark. On this particular day, which happened to be in a winter month, Nancy and I rode through the muddy vineyards and over to the park, heading right out into the undesignated area. The soil in that area of the county is composed of heavy clay, which notoriously bogs down vehicles in the vineyards and elsewhere. Riding our horses, muddy to the knees, through a narrow, secluded draw near the river we began to hear the sound of loud, high-pitched engines coming ever closer. Looking back we saw a large pickup, hurtling full speed ahead, quickly closing in on us. We were riding in a narrow area where there was no place to pull over and the banks were much too slippery to climb. Finding ourselves trapped, we simultaneously began to scream. The combination of our screaming and the screaming engines of the pickups frightened the horses who are fight-or-flight animals. They quickly bolted in fear. Coming around the corner the driver had spotted us, slamming on his brakes and crashing into the embankment. Hearing a loud crash we looked back to see the oncoming truck, sliding through the mud, with the truck behind it, crashing into the first truck. Attempting to stop our horses and thinking that we should go back to help, we heard the loud angry voices of the young men who were driving the trucks calling out to us, "We're going to kill you bitches!!!" The last thing I remember is yelling to Nancy, "Let's get the hell outta here!" and the two of us galloping full speed back to the safety of the park. It was one heck of a very muddy close call. Nancy likes to say that we've shared some "colorful experiences."

Making the acquaintance of other like-minded horse owners had created an entirely new layer of fullness within my life, helping to fill in the empty spaces that caring for my family had previously held. My every free moment was scheduled with riding dates throughout all seasons of the year, with many different riding buddies. I would ride with friends in sweltering heat or don a slicker and go out in the rain bundled up to the eyeballs to ride in freezing temperatures.

I met my friend Ishi at a meeting of a local horse club and we made a date to ride together. She rode, instead of a horse, a beautiful caramel-colored and very intelligent mule named Bonita, who had been trained in the show ring. Having never previously known a mule — only a belligerent donkey named Pedro who threw me off over his head when I was ten — I was unprepared for the stamina and sure-footed resilience that Bonita exhibited. Mules have smaller, more compact hooves than horses and can securely traverse the steepest and rockiest trails with ease. Bonita, with her long, soft ears, was smitten with my handsome black Amigo. Humorously, the minute she was backed out of her trailer and saw Amigo, she would exhibit signs of "coming into season" and could not get near him quick enough, squealing and striking out with a foreleg. He was unfazed by these shenanigans and was always glad to see Bonita. They were unfailingly compatible on the trail and at our campsites. Our pair of equine buddies made quite an impression on hikers and other riders we encountered out on the multitude of trails, over the years of our shared riding experiences. Little girls would beg to pet Amigo, "Look, Daddy, it's the black stallion." But, more often than not, people would stop to admire Bonita, asking, "What is this animal, it's not a horse, is it?"

Ishi had been the co-owner of a costume shop in Santa Rosa for many years and had also been involved with horses for much of this time. The evening we met at the riding club meeting — in the rustic clubhouse located at the rear of the Sonoma County Fairgrounds — I also met a tall, good-looking cowboy-type with a Southern accent, who introduced himself as Ron. This man was unusually attentive and flirty with me. I gave him my business card and he began to telephone. When I suggested that we might meet for coffee one day he said, "Oh I'm not sure that my girlfriend Ishi would like that." This completely took me by surprise. I repeated back to him, "Ishi is your girlfriend?" Which is when he told me that they lived together and that was that. I hoped never to see him again.

After that first meeting, Ishi and I began to meet regularly for rides and became better acquainted, but she never mentioned Ron and I was too embarrassed to tell her about my telephone encounter with him. Bluegrass music was her favorite and she suggested that we drive to Petaluma to listen to a bluegrass band, who would be playing at a pub that evening. Driving along a back road on the way to Petaluma, Ishi began to cry. She told me that her boyfriend Ron had gone home to Tennessee and how much she missed him. She went on to tell me that he had requested her to sell her business, come to Tennessee and buy out his ex-wife's share of their co-owned home there. I asked her to pull over to the side of the road and hesitantly related my encounters with Ron, knowing that this might not go so well. Ishi had owned her business for many years and really loved it. I asked if she thought selling it might be a hasty decision? My personal thoughts were these; "Well that's it, this woman will never speak to me again. Too bad because I really like hanging out with her." Ishi dried her tears, telling me that she had always suspected Ron of cheating on her. We went on to the pub and had an enjoyable night listing to music. A few days later, a card from Ishi arrived in the mail, the first of many I would receive from her over the years, thanking me for being "...such an honest woman and a good friend." Ultimately she gave Ron the axe and we became the very best of friends.

The twelve years I lived on my mini-ranch were sweet and mostly very peaceful. My life was fuller than ever. My career was going strong and paying the bills. Caring for the horses and the property and regularly attending meetings of Al-Anon, Alateen and board meetings of the various other clubs and organizations that I had become involved with, kept me plenty busy. I had also begun to go out dancing with my friend Ann. We often danced three nights a week, taking lessons and really enjoying a line-dancing class, which was great exercise. The dancing was very social and good for me, always having been naturally shy in public and having become even more so due to the appearance of my paralyzed face. The busier I kept myself, the less time I had to agonize about the health and whereabouts of my daughter, who occasionally floated in and out of my life.

Maybe halfway during my years at the little ranch, Aura came to me asking for help. She wanted to "clean up her act" and go to rehab. Michael and I had started a college fund for her when she was younger. We met at a bank and cashed it in, using the money to pay for her rehab. After much discussion about where she should go, we decided that she might as well go to the facility near my property. We would be able to have regular contact during the thirty days she would spend there. In retrospect, this was not the best idea. But — coulda, shoulda, woulda. This was not a simple process for Aura as her addictions had escalated over the years. She was now in her early twenties and had been out there on the street cultivating her various, unhealthy habits for a long time. The other clients requiring treatment included many professional people — doctors, firefighters and lawyers. Other clients included various adults, some whose parents had allowed their grown children to continue to live with them — unwisely enabling their drug and alcohol habits until their own lives had become intolerable and of course the rebellious young adults like my daughter. Young people often have the most difficult time, envisioning a long life looming ahead of them as clean and sober people, having no fun and too much responsibility.

Overcoming addiction is a daunting prospect for anyone at any age, in any walk of life, rich or poor. Because the behavior of the addict directly impacts the lives of everyone they encounter, the recovery process is often made more difficult by family members thinking that they are helping — when in fact they are prolonging the addiction. In the case of my daughter, I would have to witness the painful experience of her roller-coaster ride in and out of sobriety. Hope, however, is a powerful human emotion. Even a little hope is better than no hope. One of the most profound insights I gained from the Al-Anon program, concerns having expectations. I learned that expectations can often be the ruination of hope and that they are better avoided than harbored. This lifelong learning experience has undoubtedly saved me from a huge load of personal suffering. Today, Aura is very happily married. She and her husband share three children. She has worked at the same professional job for many years and went to school, successfully seeking an advanced degree. My relating of her story is intended only as a message of hope for all parents of the world.

Pay Attention
To Those Red Flags

Each time my friend Ann and I would pass St. Francis Winery, on our way to a dance class in Santa Rosa I would sigh, telling her how much I missed my friend Joe Martin. She encouraged me to invite him to dinner at my home. In 1988 Joe and Lloyd had partnered their interests in the winery with the Kopf Foundation, who already owned a number of prestigious wineries in their Kobrand Company. Together Joe, Lloyd and Kobrand sold the facility and houses at the small original winery site, with St. Francis retaining ownership of the vineyards for their estate wines program. St. Francis moved only a few miles down Hwy 12, constructing the impressive new California Mission-style winery and facility, placed right at the base of Hood Mountain. Joseph, with his title as founder of St. Francis Winery, still went to the winery each day. Working in his large, corner office with its panoramic views of Hood Mountain, Joe continued his hands-on association with the business. Emma, his wife of forty-three years, had passed away and he was living on his fifty-five-acre grape ranch on Starr Road in Windsor supplying grapes to St. Francis and other local wineries.

Joe and I occasionally met for lunch and then he began to invite me to dinner events at the gorgeous, new, state-of-the-art winery. One night he walked me out through the dark, moonlit parking lot to my pickup truck. I was wearing an elegant, fitted sheath dress and heels. As I started to climb up into the seat of my pickup truck, Joe basically picked me up and placing me on the seat, he leaned in and began to kiss me. I had been in love with him for many years but had never given him a clue. Even at the age of sixty-nine he was still very naïve about women in many ways. Now that neither of us was married, we began seeing each other in earnest. Finally, it got to the point where Joe, instead of going home to Windsor after work, would come instead to my place, eventually staying five nights a week. Then we would go to his ranch in Windsor to spend the weekends. We were both, I believe, shocked and surprised at how happy we were. When he proposed I said yes. He loved spending time at my place in Glen Ellen, contented to have an affectionate woman cooking and looking after him. During a discussion about marriage he said, "Well, we can either live here and sell my place in Windsor, live in Windsor or sell both places and buy one of our own. What would you like to do?" Because Joe was so casual about this, I naively didn't realize what a huge deal it would turn out to be, both legally and personally, to sell the ranch on Starr Road.

We decided to spend a weekend in Mendocino and made a reservation at the historic, Heritage House Inn. This would turn out to be the undisputedly most romantic weekend of my life. The drive from Sonoma to Mendocino is picturesque and serene. We stopped on the way at Roederer, a sparkling wine estate in Anderson Valley. Tasting some wines, we purchased a magnum of Brut and a champagne stopper. Before leaving Sonoma we had also picked up a huge bag of ripe, red cherries at a fruit stand and some snacks to bring along. The Heritage House had long been noted as a premier lodging destination in the Mendocino area — made famous in the movie, Same Time Next Year. Our rooms were situated on a rocky cliff at the edge of a small lovely lagoon, with a veranda that was cantilevered right over the endless, foamy, azure sea. The bathroom had a huge sunken tub, large enough to accommodate both of us. Although we did go out to eat and stroll around town, mostly we just stayed in our rooms soaking in bubble bath and drinking champagne, or sitting out on the veranda eating cherries and spitting the pits out into the sea — a fond memory that would resurface for many years, each time we ate cherries.

Every Tuesday Joe's dear friend Virginia hosted a huge authentic Italian dinner at her comfortable home in Kenwood. This dinner had been a neighborhood tradition for years and I was thrilled to be included in the warm local gathering. I had known Virginia and her husband Tony from the early days at the original winery, where they appeared at every party. Virginia and I were happy to reunite and soon became close friends. Prior to one of these dinners, I had dropped Joe off for a business meeting in Santa Rosa and drove away to do errands, agreeing to pick him up at a certain time. On my way back to collect him, I found myself stuck in traffic in a turning lane at a broken stoplight and was unable to cross without running a red light, through heavy oncoming traffic. My cell phone rang and it was Joe who was hopping mad. When I tried to describe my predicament and the fact that I was also frightened, he screamed into the phone, " I don't give a shit if you're scared or not. Get your ass over here now and pick me up!" Very frightened, I ran the red light. Minutes later, when I arrived to pick him up he was livid. Getting into the car, he peeled out on to the street, gunning the engine and pounded so hard on the steering wheel that I thought it might break. He began to scream, "You always make me late…." Then I remembered his stories about Emma always being late. He had told me, "Emma would never start to get ready to go until it was time to leave." This was my first inkling that he was confusing her memory with me. We arrived at the Kenwood dinner early. Aside from her son Tony, we were the first ones to arrive. This was to be the beginning of what I came to know as Joe's meltdowns. My friend Nan, the longtime PR Director at the winery was also one of my fitness clients. She was following our love affair with interest and said to me one day, "Watch out for Joe's black moods. He has a very volatile personality." They were buddies and spent a lot of time together on winery business. She went on to describe the fun they would have together, only to have the day end on a sour note because he would "…throw a tantrum for no reason at all." But I was so happy that I didn't pay much attention to the red flags of caution.

One morning not long after I had first moved to the house on Starr Road, I was storing some of my things in a cabinet in the bathroom and found a large brown grocery sack completely full of unopened diabetic supplies. Thinking that I should dispose of them, I asked if they had belonged to Emma, who was diabetic. But he told me no, they were his. Then I looked at the name on all of the unopened prescriptions and supplies and realized that this was true. I asked him why he had never mentioned his diabetes to me. Also, I had never witnessed him monitoring his blood sugar. He blithely answered that his doctor had told him that he was "pre-diabetic" and so he had stashed the bag of supplies and never thought about them again. He told me that prior to our relationship, he would eat an entire bag of peanut brittle with a bottle of wine for dinner, every night.

When Joe and Emma — both Irish and Catholic — met in San Francisco and decided to marry, he was a strapping 6'3", handsome, gainfully employed and very unworldly twenty-one-year-old. Emma was a feisty, forty-year-old divorcee with a sixteen-year-old son named Bob. As Joe later recounted the story to me, his mother who was roughly the same age as Emma, never spoke to him again after they married. In fact, Joe never spoke about his mother. He didn't even have a photo of her. His father had passed away when he was young and to the best of my knowledge, Joe did not own a photo of either of them, although an old image in an oval frame of his very stern-looking Irish grandmother, and handsome Portuguese grandfather hung in our house for years. His parents Mary (Irish — Gorham) and Antonio (Portuguese — Martines) had two boys, Joe and Tony and two girls Alice and Mary. Genetic polycystic kidney disease claimed both Joe's father and younger brother Tony as young men. Joe and Emma never had any children of their own but Joe had numerous nieces and nephews. Stories told to me by these offspring describe Joe's mother as "the monster" who apparently by all accounts mercilessly beat her children and also some of the grandchildren in fits of uncontrollable rage, the results of which I feel sure, were the cause of the regular, screaming nightmares to which Joe was prone. Perhaps his mother was bipolar? Much later his mother had another son, Paul.

When we had first begun dating, Joe, who loved to host parties in his pool house on Starr Road, hosted a large family barbeque. He inevitably wore a white chef's apron with "Joe" embroidered on a top corner, of which he owned an entire collection and in which he is depicted in numerous photos. As always, his close friends Virginia and her neighbors Bob and Jeannie were present, as well as some folks from the winery. Joe had asked me to trailer my horse Amigo along with me and ride him around the lovely pond to entertain his guests. This was my first invitation to his home in Windsor and I was very nervous about meeting his family. Dressed in a freshly ironed cowboy shirt, I made my way on my horse around the stunningly beautiful rural estate, finding my way to the large picturesque pond full of honking geese. After riding around the impressive grounds, I tied up my horse and went to the party.

As this relationship between Joseph and myself progressed, I naturally assumed — never a good idea! — his family would be pleased he had found a girlfriend, putting an end to his loneliness. It was quickly apparent I couldn't have been more mistaken. Walking into the party, I was hastily approached by a man who, without saying hello, said in a brusque and unfriendly manner, "I'm Bob, Emma's son." To which I replied as sweetly as possible while watching him stomp away as quickly as he had approached, "Oh I'm so glad to meet you. Emma was a friend of mine." Then one by one, I found myself scrutinized by the entire crowd, hands up to their mouths whispering. No one introduced themselves or asked me any questions about myself except Joe's (late) sister Alice. She immediately began to interrogate me in the voice of a fishwife, on the topic of marriage, stating frankly that the only thing I could possibly be interested in would be Joe's money. At one point I complimented her son on a delicious dish he had brought and said, "Frankie" — which was what everyone in the room was calling him — "these stuffed mushrooms are fabulous," to which he barked back, "My name is Frank. Don't call me Frankie!" It was quite clear that his family was not glad to meet me, but Joe didn't seem to notice. Later, when I voiced my concerns he said, for the first of countless times I heard him say, "Oh don't worry. My family always sees the dark side of everything." This would later become a theme in our marriage. But I didn't pay attention to the red flags. Fortunately for me, Virginia, Bobby and Jean were upbeat, warm and welcoming and stayed close to me until I collected my horse and went home.

When Joe officially announced our engagement, he threw a big family party at an upscale seafood restaurant in San Francisco. A serious seafood lover, I was anticipating the food and happy to be out with Joe. As the party was winding down I happened to overhear a very disturbing conversation in the ladies room. One of Joe's nieces was saying loudly to another niece, "…that f…..g bitch Aunt Alice …" This was a big shocker to me, as I revered all of my aunts and uncles and wouldn't have dreamed of negating a single one of them in any manner. Again, when I recounted this story to Joe, he brushed it off telling me that this niece was loud and course and to forget about it. Soon, however, I began to notice that the various factions within the family appeared to hold grudges against one another.

After WWII my Uncle Nate and Aunt Sylvia had built a spacious home on a corner lot in San Francisco, not far from Ocean Beach where my cousin Marcia was born and still lives with her husband Jim. As a small child I spent a lot of time there, living with them when my parents were in the process of moving from Southern California to San Francisco. This house is like a second home to all of our cousins and to many of Jim and Marcia's various family and friends. Joe and I were often invited to spend the night after evenings out in the city and Joe became very comfortable there with my family. Although he loved and doted on his own family members, I believe that it was a revelation to him how well my entire family got along, in stark contrast to the contentious, squabbling factions of his own family.

We were invited to a wedding anniversary party for Bob and Jean Giannini, in their large backyard, which abutted the original St. Francis Winery property's many acres of vineyards. As a surprise for them Joe had purchased airline tickets to Italy. Joe loved Italy and wanted to go on an extended trip prior to our wedding, hoping to include Bob and Jean who had relatives in Lucca. He had already booked the entire trip, making hotel reservations for a month-long trip for the four of us, without consulting Bob or Jean. They were extremely surprised and overwhelmed by Joe's generosity, to say the least. For me, this trip was a romantic dream come true. The four of us spent an entire month, driving from Milan to the Swiss border of Lake Como and all the way down to Capri in the boot of the country. This is how I came to love the Gianninis and subsequently, their entire family. In typical Joseph-style, we had only a partial itinerary, which included many gaps without room bookings. Some of these gaps actually turned out to be the most fun of all. The four of us got along splendidly, with never a cross word that I can remember, throughout the entire journey. Bobby speaks fair Italian, which was a big help along the way. We explored and experimented, meeting loads of lovely Italian people and just generally having a ball. Because of the extended nature of this trip I can't relate every single experience, but some of them stand out in my memory more prominently than others. We had flown to Milan, which is renowned for its very upscale fashion district. Many of the shops in this enchanting neighborhood were kept locked during business hours. It was required to knock and request admittance in order to enter and shop. One morning, the four of us were strolling through this charming neighborhood, Bobby and myself in front with Joe and Jean behind. Suddenly a large black Mercedes Benz shot up onto the curb knocking Bobby to the ground. I began screaming and banging on the boot of the car. An elegant silver-haired Italian gentleman, immaculately attired, rushed out of the car, to where poor Bobby lay on the sidewalk. The man was naturally distressed saying, "Oh Dios Mio, what have I done." Then Bobby got up, saying that he was ok. Meanwhile Joe and Jean were still meandering down the street. Bobby insisted that he was not injured and the Italian gentleman drove away. I don't remember hearing Bobby complaining about pain as we continued on our trip, but when we returned home he had rotator cuff surgery as a result of his fall in Milan.

Along the way, we ate the food of the gods, drank succulent Italian wines in both upscale and down-home restaurants, listened as a man sang opera in a piazza under a large glowing moon, and visited many interesting places. We stuffed our dirty laundry into cardboard boxes and shipped it home from local post offices. Occasionally we went to a local laundromat and drank espresso, while watching the clothes spin around and spent three or four days in Florence, basking in the beauty and history of this very friendly city. On our final day in Florence, Joe and Bobby went off to pick up a rental car. Jeannie and I had agreed to meet them near an elevator in the hotel where we were staying. Earlier in the day, as the four of us ambled across the Ponte Vecchio — the oldest bridge in Florence, which spans the Arno River — Joe had been praising me to Bobby. "Nancy is such a great traveler and always takes responsibility for her own luggage." He added that Emma would not have been "caught dead" pulling her own suitcase and that he always had to be responsible for every little thing. On our appointed checkout time, Jean and I were completely packed, sitting on a bench in front of the elevator door. The doors slid open and Joe burst out with a bright-red face, yelling loudly and making quite a scene. "How *dare* you leave this camera case for me to carry?" He was in an uncontrollable rage. I was completely baffled and offended. While packing for the trip, Joe had included a large, heavy camera case, with a camera that I had never seen and did not know how to use. I encouraged him to leave it at home, so that we would not have to lug it around. Bobby, who had been waiting in the car, did not witness this event. But he was noticeably upset by Joe's sudden black mood, which lasted for hours and darkened the remainder of our day. Jeannie was, at this time, in the early stages of Alzheimer's disease and was very confused by the entire incident.

After traveling for nearly three weeks, we arrived at the ancient, picturesque, village of Lucca — a walking city — where no autos are allowed inside the walls. We had no room reservations. It was already mid-day when Bobby and I went into the visitor's center to see about finding rooms for the night. We were able to find a room each, for one night only, in a historic building that had become a bed and breakfast. After checking in, the four of us took a walk, looking for a place to eat. Entering a little café and sitting down, we heard a voice calling out, "Roberto!" It was Paul, a waiter friend of Bob's from San Francisco. Sharing a good laugh at this amazing coincidence, we asked Paul if he knew of any likely hotel in the village where we could stay and continue our exploration of the Lucca area. Paul told us that his wife operated a bed and breakfast not far from Lucca, in the tiny walled, hilltop village of Montecarlo, up the Wine and Oil Road. But, he said, "It is probably not fancy enough to suit you Americanos." We asked him to call and book rooms. This turned out to be one of the most pleasant experiences of the entire trip. We encountered very few other tourists in Montecarlo — not to be confused with the famous Monte Carlo on the Riviera. It appeared that we had the entire charming little village all to ourselves, except for the local residents and shopkeepers. The bed and breakfast had formerly been an old school, lovingly restored and with few frills, it comfortably met all of our needs. We discovered Antonio's, a fabulous restaurant perched on a promontory, with huge windows hung with bright orange chiffon drapes, billowing in the refreshing breezes and overlooking the entire region. Dining there numerous times during our stay we became friendly with Antonio and his wife and even took photos of Bobby in the kitchen with Antonio. Each day we would wend our way down the Wine and Oil Road, setting off on day trips, returning back to our quiet hotel and then dining on masterfully prepared dishes at Antonio's. It was a dream-like week and we did not want to see it come to an end.

At the end of our stay in Lucca, it was time for us to part ways with Bob and Jean. Dropping them off at the home of Bob's cousin who lived on the outskirts of Lucca, we continued on alone. Driving through the seaport of Naples, we made our way down to the Amalfi Coast in the boot of the country, passing through the storied city of Sorrento. Arriving in Massa Lubrense, a tiny village located directly across the bay from the enchanted Isle of Capri, our reserved rooms awaited us. This was a family-run hotel where Mama Louisa ruled the roost. She could be found at any given time, polishing the banisters or scrubbing floors with her daughter-in-law at her side. Every inch of the hotel was absolutely immaculate. It also had a large restaurant where one could sit and sip a cappuccino or limoncello while watching the boats ferrying people back and forth, to and from Capri. On our first night there while having dinner in the restaurant, I asked the waiter what kind of fish was being served? He answered, "lo-cal" and for years afterward, each time we had fish we looked at each other and said "lo-cal." We were very fortunate to end our trip in this particular spot, because following an entire month of travel I found myself suddenly bedridden with rather severe flu-like symptoms. Not able to leave the room, I sat bundled in a blanket at the window, watching the boats ferry tourists to and fro. Our room was large and sumptuous, furnished with gorgeous Italian, antique furniture. Wall hangings and draperies of thickly textured hand-woven fabrics adorned the walls. Mama Louisa heard that I was unwell and had chicken broth with poached eggs sent up to cure me — delicious!

I discovered, along our travels, that the European *farmacia* is the very best. Throughout the trip if a health issue came up for any of us, we found that we could walk into a *farmacia* pointing to the spot on our body that was ailing us and would be given remedies that would inevitably cure the problem — pronto. Our hotel was somewhat isolated, as it was the roadside jumping-off spot for Capri. The actual village of Masa Lubrense was a few miles up the road. We had relinquished our rental car in Sorrento and ridden the bus to our hotel, leaving us with no transportation. Joe was surprisingly, uncharacteristically worried about me. He left the hotel and catching a bus bound for the little village he searched until he found the farmacia, returning with meds that fixed me right up, only to be afflicted with the same ailment himself during the night. The next day I caught the bus and repeated the trip for him. Regrettably, we never managed a visit to Capri, neither of us being well enough at the same time, having to be content with the view from afar. Finally, when we had both recovered enough to make the trip to Sorrento to rent a car, Louisa's son-in-law generously offered to drive us. Venturing on to the Naples airport, we were scheduled to catch our flight home to San Francisco. This was when things began to get really ugly. I noticed that without Bobby's constant comedy to buffer Joe's mood swings, Joe had a tendency to switch emotional gears unpredictably. On our way to the airport he went into a major meltdown, becoming more and more anxious and distressed. This was akin to watching a tornado funnel up from the bottom, becoming ever more severe and leading to an inevitable explosion. We had lost our way in Naples, which was not helping Joe's mood. Coming to a crosswalk, we needed to stop for a woman who was walking across. Joe went crazy, rolling down his window, he began honking the horn and screaming, "Get out of the way bitch or I'll kill you." Needless to say, I was terrified and hoped that the poor woman did not speak English. When we finally arrived at the airport, Joe was in a truly altered state of rage. This was when I realized that for all of his traveling and flying experience, Joe was a hysterical traveler. The main terminal was packed full in a condition of utter chaos and adding to the fact that neither of us spoke much Italian, Joe began to punch and hit me right in the middle of this large crowd. As people watched in horror, I

97

began to scream and grabbing an airport employee in uniform I said loudly in order to be heard over the din, "USA, USA!" She immediately took my hand and pulled me to the nearest door, which led upstairs through a stairwell and on to the appropriate check-in counter. Had I not grabbed her we would have surely missed our flight and who knows how I would have been able to manage Joe then? We had a twelve-hour direct flight back to SFO, during which time he thankfully slept. But I had noticed that these states of Joe's rage would often go on and on for days at a time. After claiming our luggage at SFO, we queued up with a calm and moderately sized group of folks, waiting for a shuttle to the parking lot where they could claim their cars. Joe, never one willing to wait in any kind of a line — ever — brashly rolled his suitcase right through the center of the line yelling, "Coming through! Move it!" Reaching the top of the shuttle steps he called to me to "hurry up." I was absolutely mortified and shaking my head "no," at the back of the line, indicating that I would rather wait. The waiting people were rolling their eyes and shaking their heads in disbelief and it occurred to me that my husband never, ever told me that he was sorry following one of these traumatizing incidents.

Be Careful What You Wish For

Prior to our departure, we had made an appointment at a stationery store in Santa Rosa to order invitations for our wedding, which was scheduled for two weeks following our return. We met with the stationer and agreed on everything as we often did and then Joe said, "How can we word this to prevent people from bringing their kids to the wedding?" "Easy," the wedding planner told us, "Just say Adults Only Please." After mailing the invitations, the phone began to ring incessantly with calls from his angry relatives. "What do you mean adults only, what about our kids?" Taking a call from Joe's flamboyant sister Alice, he said, "Oh, I didn't mean *our* kids," and then — unable to deal with confrontation — he handed the phone to me saying, "You talk to her." I made the mistake of telling her what Joe had requested when ordering the invitations and in addition, of also quoting Joe who had said, "There will be two hundred and fifty people at this wedding, We can't afford to feed people's kids too." Alice went ballistic, turning the onus back on to me, as if the whole thing had been my idea.

One of the things we had been very clear about and thoroughly discussed was our total acceptance of the difference in our religions. Joe's friend, who was an interfaith minister, conducted the ceremony, much to the dismay of his church friends. Naturally, two of his very close friends, who were also his parish priests, were there too. Of the two hundred and fifty adults who had received invitations to attend our wedding, I had invited seventy-five and had never met the majority of other invitees. Joe was extremely active in his parish church and with its parishioners. One of the founders of this church, Joe had contributed significant amounts of money, time and volunteer hours in his participation in the building of the church. His fellow parishioners jokingly referred to him as "Saint Joseph" and he was beloved by everyone. Every Saturday at 4PM mass he sat in the very back pew, surrounded by a group of admiring women, who the folks in the church referred to as, "Joe's harem." When word got out in Oakmont that Joe was engaged to be married, the single women of the Catholic community jokingly proclaimed to be a day of mourning. The fact that he was sixty-seven and I was fifty-six also provoked much gossip, no one apparently remembering the age differences between Joe and Emma.

We did not even consider hiring professional help with the planning of this huge wedding, except for the caterer. We made all the plans ourselves as soon as we returned from Europe and everything turned out beautifully. It was in fact quite spectacular, held outdoors on the expansive rolling green lawns surrounding the house. The night prior to the wedding had been wet and rainy, but we had a long red carpet leading from the front door of the house to the gorgeous flower-adorned altar. A crew had erected a huge white tent, which accommodated a sit-down dinner, dance floor and a band for dancing. I had made reservations at a local spa to have my nails done and get a facial, on the morning of the wedding. After we got up that morning, Joe informed me that we needed to go to Santa Rosa to a discount store to buy small candles and brown paper bags to create luminarias, which he wanted to see lining the sides of the red carpet. Protesting, I reminded him that it was my wedding day and I had plans to go to the spa in Windsor. He blew a fuse, insisting that I accompany him on his mission. He would not take no for an answer. Not wanting to ruin this very important day in my life with an argument, I went along with him, first calling the spa to cancel and promising that I would come on the following day to pay in full for the missed services. Did I consider canceling the wedding? I still had not gotten the message and got married with chipped nail polish.

When the topic of music for the wedding came up, Joe asked if we could book Bill Vitt and his band. I was surprised and inquired if he were sure that it would not bother him to have my ex playing at our wedding, even though I had not seen or spoken to Bill for a long while? Shrugging it off he told me that he knew we would have great music and not to worry about it. I called Bill to book the date who mailed back a typical music contract specifically stating that the band was to be paid in full, in cash, at the end of the event. This contract sat on our breakfast table from the time it was received until the evening of the wedding. At the end of the wedding, the customary help was paid and sent on their way. After the wedding, when Bill knocked on the front door asking to be paid, I called Joe to the door, knowing that there was more than enough cash in the safe to pay the band. But Joe was seriously drunk and began to argue with Bill rudely saying, "No way, I don't do CODs. I'll mail you a check." Bill patiently explained that the band members were always paid in full at the end of each gig. Of course, Joe knew this, but instead of going to the safe to get the cash he began to throw a tantrum, stomped out the door and drove away without saying goodbye, leaving me — in my wedding dress — and Bill along with one of Joe's nephews and his family standing there in stunned silence. I didn't know the combination to the safe at that time and I was embarrassed beyond belief. The band left without getting paid.

My new husband had driven forty-five minutes to the winery to write a check, knowing that the band would not accept one. Alone and crying, I was confused, worried and angry. He returned hours later in a complete rage saying, "Where did everybody go?" The next morning he got up and drove to the winery without so much as one word to me and stayed in this totally unreasonable state, not speaking to me for days after our wedding.

Following our wedding in the fall of 2004, we traveled a full six months within the next twelve months. Much of this travel included winery business trips around the USA, some to exciting places like NYC and other, more unlikely destinations such as Wisconsin. The Wisconsin trip stands out in my memory as one of the most interesting and pleasant sojourns that Joseph and I took together, a combination of business and vacation. I had a former client and friend also named Nancy, who had moved back to her hometown on the outskirts of Milwaukee, in a lovely home situated alongside a placid lake. We kept in touch and when she discovered that we were coming to Wisconsin on business, Nancy and her husband Mike invited us to dinner. In our rental car, we easily found her home and enjoyed a companionable evening with these pleasant folks. In our communications prior to the trip, Nancy highly encouraged us to include the little tourist destination of Fish Creek in Door County as a stopover on the trip. Researching Fish Creek before the trips I discovered it to be a charming village, akin to Cape Cod, right on the shores of Lake Michigan. I called a few places to inquire about rooms and reached the historic White Swan Inn. The owner answered the phone and inquired as to the nature of our visit, as it was occurring at the end of the annual tourist season. When I told him that we were in Wisconsin representing St. Francis Winery, he became very excited and asked if he could host a winemaker dinner at his hotel. At first I was not particularly receptive, as I had viewed this stop as a time for rest and relaxation. Pressing the issue, he finally convinced me to agree and so I booked our stay and he arranged the dinner. The drive from Milwaukee to Door County was scenic and restful. Arriving in Fish Creek, we could barely believe our eyes. The village, so charming and impressive, was positively magical! The owner of the White Swan had mentioned to me that the tourist season had come to an end the previous week. When we arrived, the village appeared to be almost deserted except for the local residents. Winter makes its entrance quickly along the banks of Lake Michigan. The chilling lake effect had already begun and the temperatures were already below freezing. People were wearing furs, parkas, and earmuffs. The White Swan Inn — as we were told — had been floated across Lake Michigan from its former location on the other side of the lake, to the current resting place. When we arrived, we could see that it was a delightful and architecturally captivating, historic hotel. Added to that, the hotel had already been officially shuttered for the season, leaving Joseph and myself as the only guests. We had the entire place to ourselves. Our rooms were unbelievably romantic with loads of gorgeous antiques and French doors with views onto the lake. We were completely enchanted. The winemaker dinner was scheduled for that first evening. Much to our surprise, a huge turnout of local wine lovers braving the weather were already seated in the sumptuous dining room when we came downstairs, waiting to meet us, and the food was great. The next morning — another surprise — the gracious owner had laid a table for us in the sunroom of the hotel, personally serving us a luxurious breakfast. Afterward, we bundled up and walking hand-in-hand, explored the entire village and nearby sites of interest. Everyone we met seemed surprised to see us out in the cold and wind. Not put off in the least by the weather, we were so happy, just wandering aimlessly around, enjoying the scenic views from every single vantage point. It was cherry season in Door County. Shops were offering cherry pies, jams and all things cherry. There was another lovely, historic hotel located within walking distance of our hotel, where we had made a dinner reservation for that evening. Walking to dinner and back in the starry darkness, with moonlight reflected on the shimmering lake, was yet another unforgettable experience. We had enjoyed a long leisurely dinner and arriving back at our hotel — chilled to the bone — we saw that the owner had set a huge roaring fire just for us in the lobby fireplace. Joe went to the bar and procured a bottle of St. Francis Merlot. Snooping around in the restaurant kitchen, I found a homemade cherry pie in the walk-in fridge. Meeting back in the lobby, lit only by candles and the toasty, blazing fire, we proceeded to devour the entire pie and polish off the Merlot before retiring upstairs in a dream-like state.

We had no desire to leave Fish Creek, but were expected at the next stop on our itinerary in Kohler at the famed American Club, to participate in the annual Kohler Food and Wine Experience. Kohler is a village in Sheboygan County along the Sheboygan River, a model company town originally built to house the numerous employees of the huge, Kohler plumbing company. Driving through this little town I was immediately reminded of the old movie, *The Stepford Wives*. It had a cookie-cutter layout and pristine perfection, with the Kohler facility and its gorgeous showrooms situated nearby. Other than the Kohler facility itself, the renowned American Club would be Kohler's other claim to fame. Upon entering our suite of rooms, I remember exclaiming, "There are awesome handmade sinks in every room. I've never seen so much china." The bathroom itself was truly a sight to behold. The entire layout of the resort and its grounds were tastefully decorated in every aspect. A massive annual wine tasting was held in the very upscale, multi-storied showroom, featuring their unique and sparkling china and stainless steel plumbing fixtures, used as props to showcase the wines and accompanying hors d'oeuvres. Each year, the facility hosting this event offers an opportunity to the public to purchase tickets, take seminars, and listen to talks on food and wine by world-renowned chefs and wine-industry personalities. Joseph offered a personal wine seminar and was also scheduled to co-host another of these seminar/food demos with Chef Walter Scheib, who was promoting his book, White House Chef (*Eleven Years, Two Presidents, One Kitchen*). Chef Scheib, a very personable and friendly man who had been the chef-in-residence at the White House through both the Bill Clinton and George W. Bush presidential administrations had endless, interesting stories to entertain the audience about these famous families. All in all, the total experience was elegant, unique and enriching and we were glad to have participated.

Our next and final stop in Wisconsin was to be a long-awaited visit with my old friend Jenny, from Ross, CA, who with her husband John now lived in Madison. The day trip from Kohler to Madison was peaceful and lots of fun. All along the roadway sat the most magnificent barns I have ever seen — "Omigosh, pull over!" — offering unlimited photo ops. Joe was amazingly patient as I asked him to stop numerous times, so that I could hop out to photograph these incredible old barns. Some of the barns housed antique shops or warehouses filled with the choicest items, from old cookware and crockery to dolls, plows and old cars. It was hard to resist this opportunity, wishing we were pulling a big trailer to load up, but we happily window shopped, buying only a few gifts.

Madison is refreshingly all-American with its mix of rural and city neighborhoods. Jenny and I have one of those relationships that can weather long absences and yet when we reconnect it seems like just yesterday when we last met. After settling in with a drink, Jenny and John took us to an old bar and restaurant in Madison for a traditional Wisconsin fish boil. People were lined up around the block to get in and the bar was packed shoulder to shoulder. The food, as I remember, was nothing to write home about, but the atmosphere and camaraderie made up for the food. The next day Jenny took us on a local driving tour. We went to a tiny cheese factory and sent home a wheel of delectable, Wisconsin cheddar, visited an art gallery and an old schoolhouse, where a woman lived and created unique, colorful handmade glass beads. A really fun stop was the Mustard Museum in Madison, where we did a mustard tasting and I bought a bright yellow, university-style pennant that says, Poupon U, which now hangs in my kitchen and induces a giggle each time I look up and see it. We visited the local, lush botanical gardens and had a fine lunch in the center of town. John and Jenny were utterly gracious and welcoming, a perfect last stop in Wisconsin.

On our way from Madison to Chicago, Joe began to complain of pain and discomfort. We were just around the corner from our hotel when he asked me to pull over and proceeded to vomit

into the gutter. He wanted to go directly to the hotel and in a
rush, I pulled into the hotel parking lot and requested help in
getting Joe up to our room while I checked in. I was very
worried, and with good reason when he passed a kidney stone.
An hour later, following a nap he proclaimed that he was good
as new and typically said, "Let's go to dinner." When we flew
into SFO, I was feeling like we had dodged a big bullet, as
Joseph had not had even one temper tantrum or meltdown on
the entire trip. The jovial and fun-loving Joe returning from a
carefree trip is the man I thought I had married and I wished
that his current state of mind would last forever.

Crazymaking

Joseph was a popular dinner guest at the various homes of his fellow church members, where we were often invited sometimes as many as five nights a week. In the early stages of our marriage, the majority of these folks were strangers to me. I had been briefly introduced to many of them at our wedding celebration, having barely a chance to chat before someone new would be hugging me, or whirling me off on to the dance floor. Even in those early days before smartphones, I always carried a handheld palm pilot device to manage our very full schedule. Having been in private practice, seeing clients on the hour for so many years, and being naturally inclined toward a sense of organization in my daily life, I always relied on my daily, weekly and monthly calendars to keep me on track. So when we began to deal with the onslaught of dinner invitations, I was very careful to notate each date. Yet an odd thing began to recur that was, to say the least, very disconcerting. Joe would come home from the winery and say, "Why aren't you ready to go? We are scheduled for dinner in Oakmont at six!" Looking at the calendar, I would tell him that I did not see an appointment for that date and also that I did not recognize the names of the people he had mentioned. He would insist that I knew these people. He saw them at church every morning. It was impossible that I could claim never to have met them. Then I would watch, what I soon began to recognize as a major mood swing, begin to escalate. Flying into a rage, his eyes taking on a weird appearance, my husband would start to scream at me, insisting that he had told me all about this event and accusing me of forgetting, offering me only minutes to get myself ready to go out for the evening. This continued to happen on such a regular basis, that I would inquire every single morning about any plans that might be scheduled for that evening. Often he would say no and then returning home later, would repeat the same pattern. Never before having been a nervous or anxious person, I often found myself trembling in fear with negative anticipation, at the sound of his car coming up the driveway. I began to insist that we keep a joint, paper calendar, consulting with Joe each morning — yet more often than not — the same pattern would reoccur, with Joe insisting that I was having serious problems with my memory. We had been invited to one particular dinner party in the Oakmont hills, at the home of some folks I had never met. As always, I would ask Joe how I should dress, casual or dressy? I distinctly remember him telling me, "Oh, just wear your jeans." When we arrived, the hosts greeted us dressed in formal black and white wait-staff uniforms and I noted with horror that the other invitees were dressed for evening. Apparently, this had been slated as a theme party. Joe had been well aware of this and encouraged me to come miserably underdressed, an embarrassing memory to this day. At other times he would advise me to wear heels, knowing that we would be out on a lawn at a BBQ, or tell me, "No one will be dressed up for this event," only to find myself underdressed again. Later he would reprimand me for being inappropriately dressed. In my new role as Mrs. Martin, it was my responsibility to look the part and I was always assessed prior to any event. I began to call for information in advance. I remember telling a friend, "This is the only man I have ever known who would advise me on which evening bag to carry" and always he would suggest which jewelry I should wear, telling me "Wow 'em with the bling."

Time was a scary issue. I became obsessive about writing down the specific times of planned events in our calendar. Consulting with my husband in the morning I would confirm that we were expected at an event, say at six PM and we would need to be leaving the house, ready to go at five. Then later, when I was in the shower, soaking wet, Joe would come charging in and yanking me out of the shower, begin to interrogate me about the reasons that I was not ready to go, even though it may have been an hour earlier than we had confirmed earlier that morning. I tried everything asking him, for instance, if I could meet him at our various destinations? No, he did not want to take two cars. Then, when his behaviors became more severe, he began to pull up in the driveway, and leaving the engine running for extended periods of time, would just sit in the driver's seat and lay on the horn until I came out. I was a nervous wreck. Nothing I did was right, although later when we had arrived at our scheduled engagement, Joe would praise me to the skies to the other guests, going on and on about what a wonderful and perfect wife he had married. Then when we got home, he would act as if nothing negative had transpired between us and want to be intimate with me.

Eventually, I began to be more angry than afraid. When he would begin to exhibit his strange behaviors I would refuse to accompany him, which infuriated him even more. He would go on to the event, telling people that I was "out riding." Every single person I would see from his church would ask me, "Joe says that you ride your horses every day. Where do you find the time?" They all thought that I was a spoiled princess. No one would ever have guessed, much less believed, that I lived constantly in fear of Joe's rage. During the first two or three years of our marriage I spent a lot of time in tears. If Joe was at home, I would walk through the endless acres of rolling green vineyards for hours on end, trying to sort things out, trying to figure out what I was doing wrong.

When Joseph asked me to marry him, he also told me that he did not like to travel alone and asked if I would consider giving up my fitness practice to travel with him. I tried to explain that this business, which I loved, had paid my bills for many years and taken a lot of time and effort to launch and maintain. I was very careful with money, had simple needs and was always completely debt free, paying my bills off each month. Then he made this offer: "When Emma and I were married I gave her an allowance each month. Would you shut down your business and move to Windsor with me if I offered you an allowance? I'll pay the bills and you will have your own money to spend as you wish and never have to worry." I was in love and trusting him, I agreed, not realizing that I should have him put it in writing. Referring my huge client load to other trainers, I put my property on the market and took my horses and my cat, Janie, to Windsor. At the conclusion of the first year, I noticed that the monthly allowance checks were no longer appearing in my checking account. Respectfully inquiring about this issue, Joe responded by saying, "I don't know what you are talking about. I never made that promise" (a statement that I later came to know well). Instead of arguing, I consulted an attorney who told me about the 'Marvin Decision'. Apparently the actor Lee Marvin had made a similar promise, but the lady in question, like me, had failed to get it in writing. The judge ruled against her. My attorney suggested to me that since I failed to get Joe's promise in writing, it would be unlikely that I would have any legal recourse. It was, "he said, she said." This is when I began to have serious doubts that I should ever believe what Joe said, or should continue to trust him. Following my humiliating, earlier conversation with his sister Alice, I had requested a prenuptial agreement before entering into marriage, so that no one could accuse me of marrying Joe for his money. Those meetings with his lawyers were extremely uncomfortable for me. In particular, the lawyer who was in control of Joe's trust, made it clear to me from the start that he was not pleased to see Joe re-marrying. This man was rude and disrespectful to me from day one and his attitude toward me continued on in the same hostile manner until the day of Joe's death.

Having sold my property in Glen Ellen, I felt somewhat secure having my own money in the bank. Early in our marriage, Joe suggested that I allow him to invest half of those funds in what he called, "sure bet" funds that he assured me would more than double my money. He being so successful and well invested, I foolishly agreed. The majority of those funds, which I came to learn were invested with friends of his, were over the course of a few years, flushed down the drain, with no return. I basically lost much of my life savings and Joe never took any responsibility, apologized or offered to help recoup any of it. Now I was financially tied to the marriage, as I had no financial recourse to relocate.

No Gray
Areas

The 2004 holidays came and went and with the changes in the seasons I learned that the Starr Road property would always be seriously affected by heavy rains and was prone to flooding. This meant that we were occasionally flooded in on both sides, rendering us unable to leave. Photos from 2005 show my horses standing on what appears to be an island in the center of their multi-acre pasture, completely surrounded by water. If only one end of the road was seriously flooded, we would usually be able to get out by driving into the pleasant little town of Windsor. I developed a fondness for Windsor when I lived there, after learning my way around. This was the first time that I had not worked on a daily basis since I was a kid. Unused to this kind of free time I kept busy attending to my new house, keeping up with many old friends and fulfilling social obligations. I was also fortunate to have some good friends with horses, who lived nearby. My friend (the late) Paulette Carroll would often meet me at Riverfront Park on Piaso, her handsome black and white Peruvian Paint horse. She and her husband lived on Eastside Road for many years and Paulette had been riding along the Russian River since long before the park was built. I had also established a very friendly relationship with Christine DeLoach, who was also a serious rider. She and her husband Cecil, who lived in Windsor, were longtime wine-industry friends of Joe's. We became close right away and rode together as much as time would allow.

Joe and I each retained many close relationships in the Sonoma/Kenwood areas where we had both previously lived for many years. A friend of mine from Kenwood is married to a dermatologist. He has an identical twin brother, a plastic surgeon, with a private practice in NYC. The East Coast brother, who was known for his work with celebrities, had written a book about his medical work and experiences. He flew out to California a few times a year to do selected surgeries at his brother's clinic in Santa Rosa. When we heard about this, Joe encouraged me to make a consultation appointment with this plastic surgeon the next time he came to Santa Rosa. Having already undergone many hours of facial reconstructive surgery — in unsuccessful attempts to normalize my face — I was not thrilled at the idea of going through it again. Any surgery is painful and uncomfortable, but surgery on the face is especially painful. But in June of 2005 I made and kept the appointment, finding myself in the waiting room of a very tasteful and upscale clinic. Both brothers were professional and charming and explained to me what the process of lifting one side of my face would entail, in order to achieve a more symmetrical appearance. This would be yet another lengthy and complicated surgery. The doctors explained to me that, at the conclusion of the surgery my entire face would be wrapped in gauze, rendering me temporarily sightless behind the bandaging and I would go home with a nurse who would stay with me for an assigned period of time. I was scheduled to have a post-op appointment three days after the surgery to remove the bandaging. After the surgery, Joe picked me up to take me home, where the nurse would meet us. He was horrified, he said, at the way in which my head was wrapped up, with large drains coming out of each side, telling me how worried he was and promising not to leave the house for "at least five days." The nurse was very kind, sleeping in the room with me, monitoring me constantly. Three days later I woke up and found that the nurse had gone, leaving me in Joe's care. Joe had then gone off to work, leaving me alone. It was the day of my post-op appointment and I had no ride to get there. Fortunately, my palm pilot was on my bedside table and my friend Ishi called to check in on me. Feeling for the phone I answered it, telling her that I was alone and needed to get to the doctor. She rushed right over and drove me to the appointment and home again. A few weeks later I shared this story with Joe's friend Virginia, who told me that some years earlier Emma had also undergone a face-lift. According to Virginia, Emma had called her, very upset, asking Virginia to come and get her and stayed with Virginia until she felt well enough to go home.

Not long after the surgery we took a flight to Manhattan, to keep a scheduled post-op appointment with my plastic surgeon. Allowing Joe to take advantage of this time, the winery had scheduled several days of business appointments for him. The medical appointment went well, the doctor assuring me all was well with my face and that I would be pleased with the results of the surgery. Each morning for the next few days, someone from Kobrand would come to collect Joe and he would be taken off to showcase the wines in shops and restaurants around the city. This left me free to wander and explore Manhattan on my own. No one really looks at anyone else in NYC and so I didn't feel self-conscious about my bruised and swollen face. The weather was temperate and so I walked for miles, soaking in the high-energy atmosphere of New York City, shopping and visiting museums. Kobrand had scheduled a very special dinner for us, in a restaurant that would normally require a booking many months in advance. Hailing a cab one evening, we arrived at the impressive Trump Tower, Donald Trump's famous landmark building, which is located on a corner adjacent to Central Park. The restaurant, Jean Georges, is named for its famed chef, Jean Georges Vongerichten who is one of only five, three-starred Michelin chefs, with the restaurant itself having been awarded five coveted stars. Joe assured me that this would be the dining experience of a lifetime and he wasn't kidding. The dining room in Jean Georges, located high up in the tower has floor-to-ceiling windows with stunning day or night views overlooking Central

Park. Anticipating elegance, I was still unprepared for the complete picture of tasteful sophistication that was the hallmark of the restaurant. Joseph, a serious gourmand, who scoured every newspaper and magazine for restaurant reviews, kept personal lists of new restaurants to visit and relentlessly watched cooking shows. He hadn't reached a weight of well over two hundred and fifty pounds by mistake often saying, "This is an expensive look." It was not unusual for us to partake in a prix fixe menu at a local restaurant such as Hubert Keller's lavish Fleur de Lys in San Francisco, one of Joe's very favorites. But at Jean Georges we had literally hit the heights. It was sensational in every respect. The folks at Kobrand had arranged everything and all we had to do was sit back and let it happen. The prix fixe menu described the serving of seven courses, but in a delirium of satiation, I felt sure that we were served many more courses than seven. Each course topped the previous awe-inspiring dish, which we were allowed to savor at our leisure. These culinary preparations, each dish the like of which I feel sure that I will never experience again, continued to be served to us, one after another throughout a long evening. When at last the dessert selections were offered, our eyes were bulging out. Joe, always up for more was, with great mirth, taking note of my reluctance to eat another bite. Here's what I remember: Standing outside on the front steps of the famous Trump Tower I said, "I think that I'm going to have to upchuck into these bushes" and Joe replied laughing, "That was the best dinner you will ever have eaten in your life and if you throw it up I'll kill you." It was a warm and beautiful evening and we walked countless city blocks, all the way across town, back to our hotel.

At home it seemed to me that Joe's ability to control his mood swings was becoming more difficult. He seemed to be perpetually in a rage about absolutely nothing. Also it became clear to me that he was unwilling to ever discuss anything relating to his feelings or our relationship, no matter how benign. He liked to talk about other people, things going on at work, church or anything impersonal. I also learned that he was unwilling to read any notes that I left for him, or to ever leave one for me. The telephone became a source of contention as he absolutely refused to take any kind of a message for me, even from a doctor. When I reminded him that I always took messages for him and was glad to do so, he answered not thank you, but "Do I look like your secretary?" In our eleven years of marriage, Joe never took even one phone message for me. Most couples seem to be able to relax within their relationships and chat about small, sometimes insignificant, quiet things. But Joe always appeared to be either wildly happy or miserably depressed, his moods offering him absolutely no gray areas of peace or calm. He had very few comfort clothes and unless he was hosting a party down at the pool house, he dressed strictly in starched, long sleeved shirts and slacks or naked in his threadbare bathrobe. When we got married, I purchased many cotton polo shirts and khaki pants for him. He wore these at my urging, but he had no comfy clothes such as sweats, or jeans. It was one way or the other. Either he was dressed, or completely undressed.

Later that summer, Joe's cousin Albert who lived with his late wife Arlene in a rural CA farming community, was hosting a family reunion. I was only just beginning to get to know this family and had not yet really had a chance to engage in much conversation with many of them. Albert, and his wife Arlene, who could not have been more welcoming, guided us to a huge spread of luscious foods outside on their patio. I was more than surprised when Joan, Joe's late brother's wife, took me aside to a quiet place and asked me if Joe had ever been abusive to me? Not sure how to answer, I asked her why she was asking this question? In retrospect, later coming to know Joan as a loving, kind-hearted woman, I was shocked when she told me that her late husband, known to have a volatile personality, had been abusive with her and she hoped that I would not have to experience that same misery myself from Joe. I was very confused. Sweet Joan had been giving me a warning.

☮

Denial

It was during this time that my husband began to talk about suicide. Any little thing would set him off and I'd hear him say, "I'm going to kill myself." Or he would point his forefinger at his temple and pretend to shoot. Finally, I told him that I just couldn't live with the ongoing threat of his suicide and that if he kept it up, I would inform his doctor. That is exactly what happened. Joe was experiencing myriad symptoms that we couldn't explain. We were together in his doctor's office while he was being examined. I took one of the nurses aside and bursting into tears I told her about the continuing suicide threats. She put her arms around me and assured me that she would speak with the doctor after we had gone. Later, Joe calmly related to me the subsequent conversation with his doctor: He was driving his car when the cell phone rang with a call from Dr. ---, who asked him if he was planning to kill himself? Joe said that he told the doctor, "Oh I would never do that, I'm a Catholic." Not angry with me, he never questioned the fact that I had indeed told the doctor. The doctor had taken him at his word and that was the end of it. That was when I began to ask for help outside the medical community. I made the mistake of speaking with a few people who were close to Joe, all of whom accused me of lying. Two of these people, C & T even took Joe out to dinner telling him that I was going to have him committed and that they were sure if Joe ever became seriously ill, I would leave him. Later, a mutual friend, who had been seated at the same dinner table at our wedding with one of these men, finally told me, "C announced across the table at your wedding dinner, 'Does anyone have any dirt that we can use against this woman (me)

— why did Joe marry her?'" Apparently this marriage had been doomed from the start — a bad omen! I very much wished that my friend had revealed this to me sooner, before I had confided in that very same, two-faced man that I obviously couldn't trust. All of this led to a witch-hunt, with one of the sectors of Joe's family denouncing and demonizing me. But much of this occurred after I was alerted to the fact that Joe had a number of bipolar relatives. One of Joseph's nephews called to check in with me on a regular basis, always asking, "How is my uncle doing?" When finally I revealed my concerns about Joe's mental health to his nephew, he told me his own story. He had been diagnosed as severely bipolar many years prior and was responsibly taking medication to help himself. Sometimes called manic depression, it was explained to me that bipolar disorder causes extreme shifts in mood. People who suffer from it may spend weeks feeling like they're on top of the world, before plunging into a deep depression. The length of each high and low varies greatly from person to person. The nephew believed that Joe's mother must have suffered from bipolarity herself, as she was known within the family as a volatile and unpredictable person with an uncontrollable temper. In the last few years of Joe's life, grand nieces and nephews were also diagnosed. I began to journal a sort of calendar of Joe's moods, discovering a pattern of highs and lows.

Joe's nephew expressed serious concern for Joe and also for me. He wanted to discuss this issue face to face with his uncle and so we made plans for him to visit us in Windsor. On the appointed day, he arrived bringing a sumptuous lunch for us to share. We had a pleasant lunch, followed by a plan for the two of them to take a ride to look at a piece of property that we had recently purchased in Kenwood. Apparently the conversation about the family's mental health did not go so well. When they got back, the nephew was visibly distressed, telling me "My uncle dismissed me." This came as a big shock to him as they had always been very close and he had assumed that Joe would at least listen to what he had to say. But, in consideration of his personal difficulties, the nephew was not yet ready to give up. Deciding to make an appointment to speak with one of the kindly priests at Joe's church, we made and kept the appointment at the parish center together, meeting with Fr. --- in his office. Once we described Joe's ability to switch personalities on a dime, Fr. ---- began to understand how, when Joe who always presented himself as Jovial Joe at church, could then become a raging abuser once returning home. This priest had known Joseph for many years and himself had witnessed personality changes and temper tantrums. He listened to all that we had to say and advised an intervention meeting, which he would guide to encourage Joe to seek medical help. First, he suggested, Joe and I would visit with the priest together and then we would set up the intervention. I regret that the intervention never took place because both Joe and also his priest became seriously ill. Unfortunately, this priest and never recovered from his illness and sadly passed away.

Joe's physical symptoms became so severe that he checked himself into Santa Rosa Kaiser Hospital where we were members. He stayed there for many days, undergoing every possible type of test, to determine what might be wrong with him. He was firmly convinced, he told me, that he was "dying of cancer." When all of the tests came back with inconclusive results, except for his untreated diabetes (no cancer), Joe asked me to have him transferred to another local hospital, where he served on the board and had many personal relationships with doctors and staff members. At the second hospital, they gave him a special private room and began to run another battery of tests, again none of which revealed any significantly negative findings except for the untreated diabetes. His doctor told me in a meeting, that my husband was suffering from severe anxiety attacks. He was released from the hospital, yet Joe was not referred to a psychiatrist or prescribed any medications to help with his anxiety. Did they fail to treat him because he was a prominent, philanthropic donor to the hospital? I will never know. Nevertheless, we received a substantial bill from the hospital, which Joe grudgingly agreed to pay.

———————

   As the 2005 holiday season approached, we were invited to
attend a holiday theatre production at Kidstreet Learning
Center. Joe had been on the board at this school for many years
and it was his favorite charity. Kidstreet, which started as a
theatre group for street kids, had become a K-6 school, whose
charter is predicated on providing high quality education for at-
risk children. The largest homeless shelter in the city is located
within a few blocks from the school, and quite a number of the
families seeking assistance at the shelter sent their children to
school at Kidstreet. The night we attended the school play, was
my first visit to the school. Going in to the theatre, a woman at
the door was handing out small packets of facial tissue. This play
was entitled *Gifts are not Enough.* Handing us the tissue and
laughing, she told us that it was a "three-hanky play." It was, of
course, a Christmas theme. One of the kids was dressed as Santa
Claus sitting in a big chair on the stage, supposedly taking place
in a department store. I don't recall there being any fancy props
or ornamentation, just a long line of bedraggled kids, waiting to
see Santa. The kids approached one by one earnestly speaking
lines like, "Santa, for my Christmas wish I ask that you help my
father who is shooting all of our food money into his arm" or
"Please Santa, my mother is a prostitute and I am afraid every
time she leaves the house that she won't come back" and "Santa,
please help my father who is an alcoholic." This was way more
than a three-hanky play, because these kids were obviously for
real and I was moved beyond belief. The very next day I went
back and signed up as a volunteer. Since the onset of my
marriage, I had been missing my Alateen experiences and all of
the great kids that I had sponsored. Kidstreet could be a new
home where I would be able to put to use all of the recovery
skills I had learned in Al-Anon and Alateen. I came to learn that

this school was volunteer-driven and the small, wonderful staff at the school was more than supportive of all of its volunteers. Very grateful to have been guided there, I seemed to fit in right away. I stayed on as a regular volunteer for close to seven years, spending one full day per week doing everything from yard duty, tutoring, teacher's aide and for many years teaching a beading class. For the last few years prior to Joe's death, I had taken our amazing golden retriever, Taffy, to school as a therapy dog.

The winery had arranged for Joe to be a wine presenter on a Mediterranean cruise ship to be sailing out of Barcelona, Spain. Flying in to Madrid, we lived through a few almost unbearably scorching hot days, the extreme heat foiling our plans to explore the city. Staying mostly indoors, we went out in the evenings for tapas and entertainment. When the sun went down, the population came out, bringing their children to play in the parks under a huge moon. A few days later after renting a car, we made our way from Madrid to the exquisite, and much cooler port city of Barcelona, down to the docks where our multi-storied cruise ship was waiting. This cruise was a mix-up from start to finish for us. When we boarded, the cruise line did not have St. Francis Winery or Mr. Martin listed on their schedule as a presenter. Later, when they finally took us to the room where myriad wines were displayed, we learned that only very few bottles of St. Francis had been delivered to the ship. Someone had not followed through and Joe was both embarrassed and furious. Neither of us was fond of large cruise ships and we sincerely wished that we had not come on the cruise. But we made the best of it, with the ship finally scheduling Joe to give a winemaker presentation. We did have fun going out on various excursions in France and Spain. Asleep in our cabin, Joe woke me up late one night wanting to talk. "Babe, babe, wake up. I need to talk to you." He began to tell me that he was feeling overwhelmed with the ongoing costs and responsibilities of operating the vineyards and property at Starr Road. He had been a grape-grower for many years and was, he said, disillusioned with the financial ups and down of the business. I asked him if he was sure that he wouldn't miss his vineyards and to my surprise, he said, "I'm so over it! Let's sell the property and go home to Kenwood." For the remainder of the trip we talked about house hunting in the Valley of the Moon where we felt we both belonged.

When the ship returned to the port of Barcelona, we disembarked with absolutely no plans at all. Inquiring about local day trips at the car rental kiosk, we learned that the favored tourist destination would be a stop at Gibraltar, located at the southern end of the Iberian Peninsula, where many Americans went for nightlife and the social scene. The opposite direction along the Costa Brava, ultimately led to the French border. Deciding to follow the Costa Brava, we passed through numerous small Spanish towns and villages. Stopping along the seashore at a fisherman's café we ate — sardines pulled fresh from the sea and grilled over an open fire — a plain and simple meal so delicious, the memory of which caused us to salivate for many years to come. Having no idea, and not really caring where we were going or would end up, I encouraged my husband to stay close to the coastline. Immediately upon entering the picturesque village of Tossa de Mar, we both knew that this is where we wanted to stop for the night. Joe went in to a modest hotel that looked promising, securing a room and for the next few days we thought that we had died and gone to heaven. I spent hours exploring the village, a maze of cobblestone streets. Charming shops with apartments above, had bright-red geraniums spilling out of flower boxes offering brightly colored wares. It was evident that the Spanish people were exceptionally clean and industrious, as every morning we would see men and women scrubbing down their sidewalks, windows, walkways and storefronts until they sparkled. Our small hotel was immaculate, the weather was perfect and the

Spanish food was divine. This was undoubtedly the friendliest country we had yet visited. Both the local people and other tourists we met were welcoming and eager to chat. We stayed on for a few days, reluctant to depart, finally deciding to continue, following the exquisite Costa Brava leading to France. This northeastern stretch of the Mediterranean is absolutely unparalleled in its majestic beauty, an irresistible photo op. The colors of the sea ranged in vivid shades of aquamarine and topaz to the deepest cobalt blues; the water so clear and pure that, standing on a cliff looking down, the ocean floor was visible. Behind us, The Pyrenees towered high between Spain and France. The beauty of Catalonia took our breath away. We were enchanted.

Our flight home to San Francisco was scheduled to fly out of an airport near Gibraltar. Joe led the way as we passed through the scanning device, placing our shoes, passports and the contents of pockets, etc., on the belt that rolled to the other side. When I went through and collected my things it was apparent that my passport was not in the tray. Trying to explain to the customs people was fruitless, as my Spanish is not good. Instead of helping me, Joe who spoke Spanish, hurried off to the terminal, leaving me to fend for myself. Finally, I found a lady behind a help counter who spoke both languages. She returned with me to the customs point and questioning the people there, determined that one of them did indeed have my passport. She thought that perhaps the man had intended to steal it and then resell it. Then this helpful woman guided me to the correct terminal where our plane was already completely boarded, waiting for me with the engines running. Rushing on to the plane, I saw Joe seated and laughing hysterically at my obvious distress. No one else on the plane was laughing. He had been ready to fly off, leaving me alone, unable to communicate and without a passport. This is when I came to the realization that my husband had a tendency to panic in airports, would never be my protector and that when traveling with him I needed to keep a sharp eye out for myself and for my belongings. It was clear that he would never help his wife.

Not long after we returned home from the cruise, it became apparent that Joe was more and more often in a state of severe agitation. Going off to work or church he would have a fine time and then returning in the afternoon or evening would become unnecessarily cruel and bullying with me. Flying off the handle for no apparent reason that I could discern — as we didn't actually fight — his rages would escalate to the point that he would sometimes refuse to speak or make eye contact with me, sometimes for as long as two weeks at a time and would never tell me why. He would demand that when he spoke to me, I should never elaborate or explain anything in any way, but should answer only in one-word responses in much the same manner as a prosecutor interrogating a witness in a courtroom. Yes or no — period. No other words were acceptable to him. This was really creepy. Reminding him that it was not his place to tell me how to speak or give me orders, he said, "I'll always give you orders and if you don't like it you can go straight to hell." The order giving became a continual, verbally abusive pattern. If I were sitting reading a book and he left the room, he would turn off the lights leaving me sitting in the dark. This was something that he continued to do for many years. He would say things like, "Nancy do you know what I really don't like about you? You read too much." Pushing and shoving was a way of life for Joe. He was a huge man who wore size fourteen shoes and had very large hands. If I were standing at the sink and he wanted something from a drawer, instead of saying that he needed a spoon, he would simply push me out of his way with both hands. When in the midst of a temper tantrum, breaking glass was another one of his scary habits. In the same way that a pyromaniac can become excited at the sight of fire, Joe seemed to react to shattering glass. When angry, he would pick up something made of glass. Holding it high over his head, he would fling it down to the floor with great force, causing shattered pieces of glass to cover the entire room. Then he would drive away immediately leaving me to clean up the mess. More than once I thought to just leave the shattered glass. This would, of course, leave our dog Taffy at risk of getting broken glass in her paws. So I was obligated to clean it up. Cooking became another serious source of contention. Although he loved and enjoyed my cooking, he started to demand to do the cooking himself, inevitably overcooking or burning the food, which would infuriate him even more. Then he would rush out to his car and drive away. Running away became his regular pattern. When things did not go as he intended, he would have a temper tantrum and leave, never telling me where he was going or when he would be back. Then he began to repeat this pattern leaving me in public places or at events.

My friend Joy and her husband had been honored with an award for their generous help and contributions to a local charity. We were invited to join them at their table, in a large hotel in Sonoma where a banquet was being held in their honor. During the presentation Joe began to sweat and appear agitated. He got up and left, without saying a word to me. I assumed that he was going to the restroom and would be right back. As the evening progressed and the event came to an end, I was humiliated to be left alone and also worried. Walking all around the hotel and not finding him anywhere, I finally approached the front desk, intending to check myself in to a room. I was too embarrassed to call my friend and ask her to come back and get me and didn't have sufficient cash for a cab. Taking out my credit card and handing it to the desk clerk, I saw Joe barreling through the lobby screaming at the top of his lungs. "Where have you been? I've been sitting out in the car — in the dark — for hours."

On another occasion during one of the holiday seasons, we were invited to a large, more informal dinner at the Santa Rosa Grange Hall, where a monk was making a presentation to raise funds for his monastery in West Sonoma County. This was a large gathering of people seated family style, together at long tables. Big platters of homestyle food were plentiful, accompanied by many bottles of wine placed on each table. I happened to be seated next to a lovely lady who introduced herself as (the late) Marijke Byck, from Paradise Ridge Winery. Marijke's special joy came from helping homeless families. We hit it off right away as she related some of her stories to me and I told her about my fondness for Kidstreet. Meanwhile, we watched Joe, who was drinking nonstop and beginning to become agitated and boisterous, causing people to roll their eyes and move away from him. When Marijke suggested to me that I ask Joe for the car keys, I did and he gave them to me. As the presentation was coming to an end, he loudly began to demand that I give him back the keys. He was making such a scene that I finally gave him the keys and he ran out the door as fast as he could. At the conclusion of the event, I found him in our car in the parking lot and asked him to please move into the passenger seat so that I could drive. He went ballistic, screaming and shouting that he would not let me drive and then abruptly drove away, leaving me standing in a dark parking lot late at night. I was obligated to ask someone coming out of the event to drive me back to Windsor, forced to admit that my drunk husband had left me there alone. The next morning, not only did Joe not apologize, he never even asked me how I had gotten home.

Although my husband would very rarely apologize for his bad behavior, he would later act as though nothing at all had occurred and say cheerfully, "Let's go out for dinner," honestly believing that this would erase whatever had occurred. Joe told me over and over that he and Emma had a saying, which they used throughout their forty-three years of marriage: "No post mortems." This meant, he told me, that once something bad happened or was said, it was never to be mentioned ever again. Pretending was apparently the way in which they avoided working out their problems. When I tried to discuss even the smallest issue, Joe would come unglued, putting his hands straight out in front of him shouting, "Babe, Babe, please!" Throughout all of the years we were married, Joe did not once ever buy me a birthday, anniversary, Valentine's Day or Christmas gift. Then, weeks or months later when we were out shopping, he would ask me to pick out something for myself for the missed event. Sometime he would get me a card and put exactly the same amount of money into it that he would send to a niece or nephew, saying, "Emma always wanted to buy her own gift," or when I presented him with a gift he would say, "Oh, sorry I didn't get you anything." Joe and Emma had no children of their own and he would spend hours, picking out cards and writing checks to the vast list of relatives and other folks to whom he regularly sent money. Well known for his generosity, he even volunteered to pay for one of the office workers at the winery to have her teeth straightened. Joe had initiated very substantial college funds for every one of Emma's grandchildren and great grandchildren as well as his own nieces and nephews and their children and was also fond of giving money away to people he had just met.

My friends and especially many of my family members began to express their concern for me. Joe had begun to beat me up in bed as we slept. We went to see a psychotherapist at Kaiser, who told him that I needed to be sleeping in a safe place, in a separate bedroom. Whenever I made plans to leave and come back to Sonoma Valley, somehow he would always charm me out of it. Although Joe claimed to disavow astrology, he was very proud to be a Gemini. Like a wound-up spring, my husband's constantly conflicting emotions would seem to bounce off of one another. As his obvious personality duality became more and more evident, I was convinced that he was suffering from bipolarity like his nephew and asked him to see a doctor. A family friend recommended a psychiatrist who then prescribed medication for bipolar syndrome. He would go on and off of the meds, exacerbating the stress to his system and causing additional strain on his already compromised heart saying, "I don't need to take that, my doctor says that I'm perfect." He also had a close personal relationship with Comet cleanser. One thing I learned early on in my marriage was never to suggest something that I would not want my husband to do, or not do. He would immediately do it just to get a reaction. A good example of this happened after we purchased a pricey new barbeque. The man who sold it to us told us never to use anything abrasive on it"...in the same way that you would not scrub your cast-iron cookware with cleanser." We cooked on that barbeque exactly one time and the next day Joe scrubbed the entire surface off of it — using multiple cans of cleanser — leaving it basically ruined. While he was by no means a clean-freak, Joe would spend long periods of time at the sink scrubbing every piece of cast-iron cookware with cleanser.

Although the Starr Road property was a showplace, I never felt that I belonged there. It was not my house or my home. Acting on Joe's wish to move back to the Valley of the Moon, I began to look at real estate there. One day in 2007, I followed a road in Kenwood, which I had never known existed, to look at a house that was listed for sale. One look told me that this would not be the house of my dreams, but turning around in the road I noticed a tiny sign nailed to a tree, which said, "probate." This opened onto a huge green, sunny meadow, with a small decrepit cottage completely surrounded by giant trees. I realized that I must be on the back border of Annadel State Park — now Trione-Annadel State Park, in which I had spent countless hours meandering on horseback. Calling a realtor friend of mine, we determined that this was a four and a half acre piece of property that had been in probate for some time. Bringing Joe back the next day, the very first thing he said was, "This is home, let's buy it." He was very excited and got right to work researching the property.

A Life
of Excess

Joe discovered a local company called Glen Ellen Packaged
Homes. They offered many different sizes and designs for
homes that were partially pre-manufactured to specification and
delivered to your site, at a price significantly lower than a
standard stick-built home. Since this was to become our
retirement home, we both felt the need to downsize from the
huge ranch at Starr Road. Four and a half acres seemed just
perfect for the house and my two horses and allow me nearby
access to ride right into the park. I was thrilled at the thought of
coming home to the valley where all of my friends and the
various organizations I belonged to, were located. Asked to
choose a home model, I chose a modest, one-story home. Joe
immediately vetoed that choice and instead placed an order for
the largest, single-story model available. It was 3,300 square feet
plus a three-car garage. He then enlisted the help of our architect
friend Neil Peoples, who had designed the new St. Francis
Winery, to customize the plans. The house would include a five-
hundred-square-foot fitness room so that I could go back to
work as a Pilates instructor, the garage, and a giant pantry and
wine room. I must emphasize the fact that I did not make any
requests for the fitness room, or any of the improvements that
came later. My only request was for a modest horse barn and
some fencing. A few years later, Joe would be diagnosed as,
among other things, "manic compulsive-obsessive," meaning
that once an idea was formed, he was powerless to stop until he

saw it through. Watching this building mania unfold was akin to watching a powerful freight train. Spending hours on end sketching plans on graph paper and ordering endless goods and services, no expense was ever spared. I tried in vain to reason with him saying that we did not need the most pricey building materials or …, yet he would spend all day, every day, on the phone asking for quotes and in the end always ordering the most expensive items. I did not want to appear ungrateful, yet I was very concerned about the huge bills. Added to this was the fact that his very unfriendly trust attorney who monitored the spending of every cent, was constantly breathing down his neck, chastising him for his extravagance. In all fairness, the fact that our house was one of the few remaining standing in our neighborhood following the horrendous Nuns fire is — I feel sure — due to the pricey metal roof and other defensible building materials that were used during construction.

There were a number of trusts, created by Joe and Emma before she passed away. Her trust was irrevocable. Joe had a large fortune contained in five trusts, some of which were irrevocable and some not, but I was always told that *all* of the trusts were irrevocable. This is what I was led to believe when we were married and continued to believe until we began to build this house — when he told me that it was his money and he could spend it any way he wanted until he died.

We were still living in Windsor, when the phone began ringing with calls from people asking me to pay their bills, which apparently were overdue. Men I had seen working on the property began ringing the doorbell, telling me that they had not been paid and wanted their money. Knowing all of this made Joe even more anxious. He announced that he planned to take out a $450,000.00 mortgage on the new Bristol Road property. This was alarming, but he assured me that I would not be personally responsible to the mortgage, should anything happen to him, for no more than one half of this sum. He intended to spend the other half cleaning up the unpaid bills at Starr Road. Every time we had made an agreement, or he made a promise, Joe would inevitably renege and tell me later, "I never said that" or "I don't remember that" or "promises are meaningless." Saying these things was his way of absolving himself from commitment or guilt. He arranged the mortgage deal quickly and was extremely agitated on the way to the title company, telling me that he had written a very large check to ---- which was not covered by sufficient funds in his checking account. He needed to get that money into the bank before the check bounced. When we arrived at the title company and they set out the paperwork for us to sign, I produced a document, stating exactly what Joe had previously told me about his plans for the use of the funds and my responsibility to the mortgage. I requested a notary public, informing the loan officer that I was unwilling to sign the mortgage paperwork until my document was signed and notarized in her presence. He was furious but we completed the process and then signed the mortgage agreement.

After that, unbridled spending on the Bristol Road property continued at a heated pace, until the main house was finally completed to Joe's satisfaction. Throughout this process, he failed to ask for my approval or consult with me about spending, or anything else. But, as he was colorblind, I was asked to choose the paint, tile and granite colors and we chose the flooring and wood for the cabinetry together. The contractor he chose for this project happened to be his late wife's, granddaughter's husband. This step-granddaughter insisted that her husband be paid on a weekly basis and she would sometimes appear in tears begging for an advance. Shortly after we were married, Joe began to give me warnings about this step-granddaughter. "Don't ever trust her or anyone in her family," he told me over and over. Apparently, his relationship to Emma's son's family had been tumultuous for many years and he had nothing good to say on this topic. Yet, when I asked him why he had hired her husband as our contractor, he told me that if he wasn't paying him on a regular basis, they might lose their own house. The housing and building market was at a standstill, with many contractors out of work and suffering. He admitted that he had a love-hate relationship with the step-granddaughter. This, I came to recognize as a symptom of the pattern of Joe's duality. He was a mass of contradictions in the entirety of his life, doing and saying opposites. His extreme need to be liked by absolutely everyone rendered him unable to make clear decisions or take a stand when it was necessary. Holding everything inside, unable to express himself appropriately, his emotions would always, finally boil over into a storm of fury. There was no gray area.

Joe was still going to work at the winery each day and as I was not working, at his request, I began to go through every drawer, room and closet in preparation for packing. He inspected every item, pricing each one himself. Many of the items purchased by Emma were brand new and still in the box with the original price tags — things like Waterford crystal candelabra and costly linens. Then we had a massive estate sale.

In anticipation of the forthcoming move into our beautiful new home, Joe and I sat down together and created a final punch list for the contractor. The first two items at the top of the list were: 1. All horse fencing completed and 2. aviary completed, as we had a small flock of rescued cockatiels and planned to adopt more. The list went on from there, since we naturally could not leave without our animals. Then I called and scheduled the movers. I had personally boxed and packed the majority of our belongings, a huge undertaking. Although we had jointly redecorated the family room adjacent to the kitchen, the remainder of Joe's home was, as he told me only after we were married, to remain the same. I learned that if I misplaced a fork in the wrong drawer there would be hell to pay. Much of my own personal furniture, etc. had been in a storage unit for the previous five years. When moving day arrived, we followed the van to Bristol Rd., where I was horrified to discover that no horse fencing had been installed and the aviary remained incomplete. Joe was unapologetic, telling me that it was more important for the towel racks and drawer pulls to have been installed. As they unloaded the van, I directed the movers to place labeled boxes in appropriate rooms. I found the box labeled "bedding" and after throwing a pile of clean folded sheets onto the bed, went back to Starr Road to continue caring for the horses, birds, dog, and cat. There was no furniture, television, food or much of anything left in the house. To say that I was angry and humiliated would be an understatement. On the twelfth day after no word from my husband, alone with my animals and my cousin Barbara who — very worried — came to stay with me, Joe appeared. He announced that the fencing and aviary were ready and as usual, acted as though nothing at all had happened. Loading up the horses and the birds, I drove to Bristol Road and put them away in their new homes. Coming into the house, I saw that instead of putting the sheets on the bed, Joe had been sleeping on the bare mattress the entire time.

The new house being mostly complete, the original little cottage was then gutted and work was begun restoring that structure, which was to be my jewelry studio. During the course of this remodeling, Joe's manic tendencies escalated to an entirely new level of compulsion. No expense was spared on the restoration to either the exterior or the interior. Checking in at the cottage, I was told that a gas line had been run to the studio for my silver kiln, which in fact is electric. But of course, no one ever asked me. Again, without my knowledge, blowers were installed into the walls to blow all surfaces clean. Had I been consulted before going to this expense, I would have explained to him that a jeweler collects every minuscule scrap of silver or gold for reuse and would never use a blower in their space. This total lack of communication manifested in the form of an intensely controlling nature, adding countless unnecessary dollars to our bottom line of expenses. I tried discussing this with the various contractors on the job, but they insisted that Joe was the boss. Naturally, the more work they did, the longer the job would go on and the more they would get paid. When the interior of the little cottage was completed, I went to the storage unit to collect my belongings, which I had not seen for quite some time. It was like Christmas, seeing my mother's beautiful old, pristine Ethan Allen furniture, her china, and silver. Carefully stacking the many boxes, I was excited in anticipation of seeing my daughter's old baby pictures and the many treasures I had collected over a lifetime, only to discover the next day that Joe had ripped open each and every box, scattering the contents around on the floor. I felt violated, as if a burglar had been there. The contractor came in to apologize for Joe's bad behavior, saying that he felt very bad watching Joe tear through my things. Then my husband came in and told me that everything I owned was "worthless." I just didn't know what to say, repacking and sealing up each box again. I was told repeatedly that everything he was doing on the property, and all of the money he was spending, was for me. The jewelry studio was intended to be my domain, yet many of my suggestions for its completion were dismissed. I had created a floor plan and drawing for the placement of the furniture in this small space and spent a pleasant day decorating it accordingly. When Joe came in and saw that I had done this he came completely unglued, screaming and shouting, throwing and breaking things and began to roughly push the furniture around, creating large, deep scratches in the brand new hardwood floors. It was terrifying to witness his compulsion to control every little thing.

Then he set to work, giving instructions for the outbuildings. The exorbitantly priced roofing materials he had insisted on using for the two houses, was also placed on an inexpensive tool shed, used only to store paint cans. Then the electrician was instructed to put pricey electrical outlets on both the inside and the outside of the shed. This went on and on for over a year after we had moved into the house, with his ideas for new projects coming every single day. Workers came with graders at great expense, to create a place for the barn to sit, without consulting me, or discussing the plan or the outcome. He instructed them to create a flat space with a berm on one side and which went steeply down on the other. This was completely inappropriate for horses as there was no way that they could get in or out of their stalls without going straight down a steep loose dirt hillside. In the end he realized his mistake and had another pad graded on a flat space at a tremendous additional expense. The barn was the last structure to go up. I had chosen a pre-fab, three-stall, all-metal barn and Joe had added a workshop for himself that would run the entire length of the back of the barn. Again, the pricey matching roofing was installed. No expense was spared. I have been caring for horses all of my life and although Joe had minimal experience with horses, he made the majority of decisions without consulting me, some not so good. But having a barn had been a dream throughout my life and I was more than thrilled. My horses had seen recent, severe winters with minimal shelter and I felt that they deserved some comfort. Once completed, Joe turned to the empty graded pad up the hill from the barn. I decided that the only sensible and economical thing to do would be to erect a small pipe-corral arena on the flat surface. Before I knew it and with no mention to me, the electrician had erected twenty-foot-tall lighting towers and a sprinkler system all around. I don't remember ever turning on either the lights or the sprinklers. My husband would tell me repeatedly; "I'm doing all this for you. All for you, I'm doing this all for you." I was living in paradise, in the home of my dreams with a totally unstable husband and no one would help me, help him.

———————————

In the fall of 2012 we planned to meet our friends Don and Mary in Perugia, Italy to spend a few weeks in a villa belonging to their friends. The issue of Joe's mental health had by this time, escalated to such a state, that many of my friends were aware that I planned to file for divorce when we returned. I was not looking forward to this trip. Joe's physical health was less than optimal. Months in advance of the trip, Don and Mary encouraged him to begin a mild walking program. Joe refused. I asked him daily, "Let's walk to the mailbox. Just a bit of exercise is better than none." He would respond with the standard answer he would give for just about everything, "I don't want to and you can't make me." Each day I would train clients in my fitness studio and Joe would sit right on the other side of the wall watching television, nonstop. No one could understand this paradox.

Suddenly, Joe seemed to be very busy cooking up a new project. He was compulsively sketching and measuring. Then shipments of very fancy kitchen hardware and plumbing fixtures began arriving on our doorstep. He confided to me that he planned to construct an outdoor kitchen in Bobby's backyard. The two of them belonged to a large men's group of local guys. Many were grape growers, or otherwise connected to the wine industry. Each month they would put on a big barbeque and cook for each other, rotating from one member's home to another. Some had fancy outdoor kitchen set-ups and others did not. But here's the clincher: Joe planned to construct this kitchen in secret, without consulting Bobby. "How," I asked him, "do you plan to do construction in Bob's backyard without his noticing?" Bobby's roses are his pride and joy. Joe planned to dig up the roses and put the outdoor kitchen in place of the flowers. Eventually, I noted that he had spent around $10,000.00 on fixtures, appliances, cabinetry and even very fancy glass tile for a backsplash. He had also ordered a custom made, stainless steel stove hood, at great expense. At this point, I convinced him that we should have Bobby and his son Tommy over for dinner, so that we could let them know what Joe was planning. After dinner I said, "Why don't you take the guys out into the garage and tell them about your new project?" What could he say? When they got a look at all of the stuff Joe had purchased and heard his secret plan, Bobby began to cry. Not only was he terribly embarrassed that Joe would spend all of this money without consulting him, but he was really angry and asked him to send it all back. Joe's immediate response was, "I'm going to kill myself." Then he turned to walk back into the house. "Hey, wait a minute," I said, "your very best friend is standing here crying and you turn your back and walk away, feeling sorry for yourself. Why don't you wait until after dinner to kill yourself?" Eventually, much of the stuff was returned, lots of it was given away and I donated the stove hood to Habitat for Humanity.

We flew out of SFO, arriving at Fiumicino Airport near Rome on October 20, very weary. The ride to Perugia was, thankfully, uneventful. Pulling up into the driveway of the lovely Italian villa, we were greeted by the colorful profusion of flowering plants and expansive views surrounding the property. The owners, a husband and wife who lived on the ground level, came out to welcome us and take us upstairs to the guest apartment where we would stay. Don and Mary had been guests here during their travels, off and on for many years. They showed us around and we settled in. Don told Joe to be sure and only use the walk-in shower in their room. The hall bath for our use had a claw-foot tub and a Plexiglas-enclosed shower above. A few days later, we heard a loud bang. Joe had climbed into the claw-foot tub and fallen out, hitting the back of his head on the tile floor. Don rushed us to Perugia hospital.

Not wanting to, or having the energy to write the story over and over, I sent the following email out to friends and family.

Following three fun-filled days in the Perugia area, Joe slipped and fell out of the bathtub/shower, landing on his back and hitting the back of his head hard on the tile. We took him immediately to the hospital in Perugia, where he stayed for 3 nights and 4 days. They did not have any available rooms and he lay on a gurney in a brightly lit, noisy crowded hallway for 2 days in his clothes. This was a teaching hospital and Joe was given a multitude of tests, including a cat scan. The doctors told me that the CAT scan showed a "fractured atlanto-occipital vertebrae with a bone shard." They put a large orthopedic collar on him, which he said made him much more comfortable. His headaches were terrible and he was given pain meds. They would not *administer an MRI — they told us — due to an old injury. The food was inedible. They would give him pills, but no water, as you were required to buy and bring your own water. On the fourth day, after he had hounded me to take him back to the villa where we were staying with friends in Colombella, and being told that there was nothing else they could do for him, they released him "with reservations." Meanwhile, our friends Don and Mary had spent days driving me back and forth to the hospital, through heavy traffic, paying around $9 per gallon for gas. This was not how they had anticipated spending their well-planned vacation.*

I put Joe to bed when we returned back to the villa, where he was thrilled to have decent food to eat. He got a good night's rest and woke up saying that he felt much better except for the headaches. I felt that we should return home to the US immediately and get him into a hospital. A retired pilot friend of Don and Mary's who lives nearby, switched our tickets. A driver took us to the Fiumicino Hilton, which is adjacent to the airport in Rome.

That night Hurricane Sandy struck and all flights were canceled. The hotel was packed with people who were stuck. Now I needed a new flight. The only time I left Joe was to go to the airport where I seemingly walked for miles and took two shuttles to get to a provider who could give us a flight. Had I waited any longer, who knows how long we would have had to stay there? As it was, the first flight out was four days later. So we hung out in the hotel, where, by the way, their credit card ATM ate my Visa card.

Our flight out of Rome had a one-hour layover at CDG Airport in Paris. We were on wheelchair access and were taken to the wheelchair area where they had run out of wheelchairs. Refusing to allow us to walk to the terminal caused us to miss our flight. This was unbelievably stressful and we were furious. We were taken, with Joe in a wheelchair, to the Air France counter where they apologized and put us up in a nearby hotel and given new boarding passes for the next morning. So we were driven to the hotel in Roilley, where we had the very best meal of the trip thus far and went to bed.

Early the next morning we got onto a shuttle to go to the terminal. It was dark and raining. Joe had trouble getting off of the bus. Stepping down, he slumped over the guardrail with traffic rushing past on the other side of the railing and said that he was unable to go on. A man in the street took one of his arms, me the other and we walked him across the busy street. Somehow we managed to get Joe in and out of an elevator and sat him in the nearest chair in the terminal, where he immediately had, to my ultimate horror, a massive stroke. His entire right side, arm and leg went numb and I can't explain how his eyes looked, but it was terrifying to watch. He couldn't see, speak or move and was slumped over in the chair. I was calling for help but no one would help us. I ran to an information station saying that I had a medical emergency and needed a wheelchair asap. During the next thirty minutes before the wheelchair arrived, I was in a complete panic. When the wheelchair attendant finally arrived, he took us to the airport medical facility. One French-speaking doctor was on duty and got Joe onto a gurney. His advice was this: go to the American Hospital in Nice for an MRI, or get on our scheduled flight. Although Joe was barely able to speak, he indicated to me that if they wouldn't give him an MRI in Perugia, they probably wouldn't do it in France either. He kept saying, "get me on the plane!"

The wheelchair guy took us through security, straight to the gate where they were holding the plane. Putting us on first, delayed the flight for close to an hour. Once in his seat, Joe was completely paralyzed and unable to walk or to get up to use to the bathroom. The entire twelve-hour flight was an unspeakable nightmare, especially knowing that we would miss the four-hour stroke window of time to receive the appropriate medication. I did not take my eyes off of Joe and asked the man in the next seat to wake me if I went to sleep. The crew pampered us in every way that they possibly could and had an ambulance waiting on the tarmac as the plane touched down at SFO. The EMTs came onto the plane with a gurney and put us into an ambulance bound for South San Francisco Kaiser. They took a cat scan and told me that they could not see any neck injury, but confirmed that Joe had indeed had a stroke. After a few hours they put us into another ambulance where we arrived at Kaiser in Santa Rosa at about 10:30PM, where we had no luggage or a car and my phone was dead.

When I saw my husband, helpless in the throes of a massive stroke, I instantly and physically felt all of my anger and resentment toward him washing away in that moment. This was my husband and it was my job to get him home.

The End
of Our Privacy

Joe was treated and evaluated at Kaiser in Santa Rosa for three days and then transferred to Kaiser in Vallejo, where he was to remain for twenty days. The huge state-of-the-art facility in Vallejo has an entire floor dedicated to stroke and spine injury patients, including two large gym facilities. A schedule is created for each patient, who is pushed to the limit throughout each day. A typical schedule might include an hour of physical therapy, an hour of occupational therapy, an hour of speech therapy, a visit with a doctor or psychotherapist, lunch and then a repeat of the previous activities. Even in his debilitated state, Joe did not like being told what to do and he flatly refused to eat. After the first couple of days had elapsed, I received a call from Dr. B, the head of psychotherapy. "What can you tell me about your husband's mental health? I notice that he is not currently prescribed any mental health medications." I told her that his nephew had revealed to me, what appeared to be a genetic family pattern and also that I had been journaling Joe's bizarre behaviors for years. She questioned me on the phone for quite some time and then called again a few days later. This time she had determined a diagnosis. Joe was, she explained, "bipolar, with dual personalities — public and private — with manic, obsessive-compulsive disorder." This diagnosis was not a surprise to me and in fact validated my own suspicions. Since the time of our marriage, Joe had been telling me that I was crazy and when I attempted to find help for him, his family and those closest to him had called me a liar.

I had been informed at the hospital, that when Joe came home, he would require a twenty-four-hour caregiver. Since he was such a large guy, it was suggested that a man who would be able to handle heavy lifting would be the best solution. Many people at the church had personal caregivers and asking around, I was given a referral from a friend of Joe's. The caregiver, J, had been with a local family until the time of the husband's death and came with high recommendations. I arranged to meet with him at a neighborhood coffee shop and hired him. He would sleep in my bedroom to be close to Joe and I would move into my art studio.

First I needed to purchase some soft, washable clothing for Joe's comfort in the hospital. Then, every day I would make the one-hour drive to Vallejo, bringing something that I hoped Joe would eat, along with clean sweats and t-shirts. Stroke victims typically have a problem swallowing. They need to eat soft foods and thickened liquids or else they can choke or aspirate. Joe was mostly unable to eat the foods that he requested and so he just refused to eat and quickly began to lose weight.

This hospital required that the spouse and/or caregiver stay for one entire day, working and learning alongside the patient, before being given a release to go home. After twenty days, hanging out at the hospital, I had become very familiar with the program and the various therapists. The day prior to Joe's release, J came to the house with his belongings and we made the final trip to Vallejo together. We spent the day learning various safety techniques for wheelchairs. There was an actual car — cut in half — in the gym. We learned how to transfer a patient from a wheelchair, into a vehicle. They had a model apartment with a bathroom, and we learned how to help the patient get on and off of a toilet and into the shower. Fortunately, our house was built on one level, had few steps and was already equipped with grab bars. The next day, we came back to collect Joe and bring him home. Our neighbor Darryl asked if he could come with us and so there were three of us there to pick him up. The hospital had provided a walker and wheelchair and the rest was up to us. Joe was now taking meds to ease his bipolar tendencies and was somewhat easier to reason with. Once a person has attained Medicare status in California, the state medical system takes charge of that patient. In order to avoid any instance of elder abuse, home nurses are sent on a regular basis to carefully monitor each patient in the first weeks after discharge from a hospital. A schedule of health workers now came in and out of the house on an hourly basis: a nurse, physical therapist, speech therapist and occupational therapist. Any previous modicum of cherished privacy had gone out the window. Each of these therapists left a packet of instructions for Joe to work with, until their next visit. Joe routinely ignored each and every suggestion for improvement. When the physical therapist first arrived and saw our fully equipped gym, he was ecstatic. Bringing Joe into the gym and guiding him through a gentle rehab program — exactly the same things that I did with my clients — he seemed convinced that Joe would soon be walking. Joe, however, stubbornly refused to allow me to help him in any way with his rehab program and the PT did not have much better luck. Joe would say, "I don't want to and you can't make me." After a few visits, the now deflated PT literally threw his hands up into the air telling me, "If he will not do anything to help himself, then there is no reason for me to be coming here." He didn't come back. Still unable to walk, Joe was much more concerned about his inability to be verbally understood. In some ways, nothing had changed. Although he slept in a hospital bed, he still sat in his chair, in front of the television, from morning to night, giving orders. The big difference was, when he had a tantrum he couldn't run to his car and drive away.

At first, the caregiver J was a model of caring and compassion. Joe had numerous physical problems, requiring constant attention and J seemed like the perfect person to help him. A former military man, he showed me with pride his certificate of completion for having earned a black belt in martial arts. He was formidable in stature and demeanor, and I felt safe having him in our employ, looking after Joe. Although I was sleeping in my art studio, all of my clothes and belongings were still in the main house. Having J looking after Joe allowed me the freedom to buy groceries, do errands and even occasionally get out on a horse. This was the time when I began walking three miles each morning so that I could try to get my head around what was happening in my life.

J began to ask me if it was ok for him to go out for a few hours in the evening after he put Joe to bed. Even though he was on a salary, not an hourly wage, I thought that it would be good for him to get some time alone. I would come up and sit with Joe, who was basically helpless in his hospital bed. When J began to stay out all night and come home drunk at dawn on a regular basis, I was alarmed and exhausted. Attempting to speak with J about his behavior did no good. He became very angry and intense, arguing loudly with the clear intention of scaring me. One morning after he had been out again all night, I told him that his behavior was unacceptable and that this would be his last day on the job. He flipped out, saying that he needed at least thirty days' notice and harshly informing me that he would not leave. All of this I kept from Joseph, not wanting to worry him. Going out for my morning walk, I was crying, not knowing exactly how to handle this large, threatening man. My neighbor Darryl happened to be out in front of his house. Noticing me crying, he sat me down and insisted that I tell him what was wrong. At the end of my story he said, "This is what I want you to do. Go home now and go into Joe's office with him. Tell him what has been going on. Then I want you to write J a check for an entire week's work. Don't leave the room." Within fifteen minutes Darryl was there with one of his workers. He came in to get the check from me and told Joe that everything would be ok. When Darryl came back, he said that J had packed up and gone. Darryl told J that he should not, under any circumstances, ever come back. I got right on the phone and called a caregiving agency, arranging for a new helper the next morning.

The agency sent D, a bubbly and perky woman in her 50s. The agency would be in charge of D's paychecks and we would work together to schedule her hours. Joe had informed me that he was only willing to pay for four hours of help three days a week. So we scheduled her hours from 9AM to 1PM, during the times I would be in the fitness studio with clients. D got Joe up, gave him breakfast and lunch and drove him to church and medical appointments. This meant that I was his full-time nurse on days when there was no caregiver scheduled and from 1PM until the following 9AM on the three days after the caregiver left. The good thing was; I got to move back into my bedroom and sleep in my own bed instead of the awful foldout couch in the art studio. The bad thing was; now I was basically chained to the house, as Joe could not be left alone. Soon enough, I noticed a pattern begin to repeat. The formerly cheerful D became sullen and argumentative. Even Joe noticed that she spent countless hours playing games on her tablet. In addition, they would watch shows like QVC together. She had his computer passwords and they began to order merchandise that we did not need. She told me, "He is my boss and I need to do what he asks," dismissing my requests that she stop making purchases for him. Although Joe was taking medicine to curb his manic tendencies, it mostly dulled his anger. I no longer had to clean up the shards of broken glass following his rages. But his basic personality remained the same. He was compulsive-obsessive. It looked like D also shared this trait with regard to shopping and other things. It was not a good mix! She would go through drawers in our bathroom and search through our refrigerator and pantry for items with expired sell-by dates and throw things out without consulting me. Her behavior became generally pushy and unacceptable, until finally I called the agency and asked for a replacement.

The agency had sent B on occasion when D was not available. Now she was assigned as our regular helper. She was a humdinger! Her regular byline regarding herself was: "If I only had a brain." But she was very good hearted and this seemed like the most important thing, in this ultra stressful time. Joe had a wound that would not heal. Eventually, he needed to go to Kaiser three times a week to have it treated. Handling B's schedule with the agency, scheduling all of Joe's medical appointments and making sure that his prescriptions were filled, was a full-time job in itself for me. I often coordinated his Kaiser appointments with times when B would be working so that she could take him and I could see clients or do some errands. Repeatedly, Joe would tell me that B was unable to ever remember the route to Kaiser — a short drive from our house. Yet he looked forward to going out with her, because he could order her to drive him around to discount stores, where he would stock up on dented canned goods that we did not need. B also took him to church and became friendly with some of Joe's church friends. Before long, it appeared that she had claimed ownership of him. My friends from the church reported to me that she incessantly gossiped about our personal business. I was not too concerned about this. Going to church was his social life. Numerous people in this elder community church had caregivers who would bring their charges in wheelchairs. Life went on in a daily pattern of medical appointments and responsibilities. My personal life had come to a complete standstill. For two years I was unable to go out at night, unwilling to leave Joe alone. Riding my horses was a thing of the past and seeing my clients became my entire social life.

In the last years of his life, Joe repeatedly injured himself, taking many falls. At the hospital in Vallejo, there was a sign over his bed that said, "Impulsive Patient." On every occasion, Joe would — even in his disabled state — do the most dangerous possible thing. Our neighbor Darryl came to the house at all times of the day and night to help me get him up off of the floor. His death certificate states, "multiple vertebral fractures" as his cause of death. Walking into the hall bathroom one day I was stunned to see Joe up on a ladder, inside of the floor-to-ceiling, glass-encased shower stall. How he had gotten himself up that ladder, I will never know. When I saw this accident waiting to happen, all I could say was, "I'm going to pretend that I don't see this," turning around and leaving him to the compulsive behavior that I was unable to understand.

In the early stages of the stroke trauma, our number one goal was to try and keep Joe's blood sugar under control. They had been giving him insulin injections in the hospital and we were instructed to carefully monitor his blood sugar. This was made much more difficult, as his family members would bring sugary desserts without consulting me first. As time went on and he lost interest in eating — but would watch cooking shows on television, day and night — his weight decreased dramatically and with the weight loss, the diabetes symptoms disappeared. Then we were begging him to eat. His doctor sent us to a specialist who discussed with him, the process of inserting a feeding tube. After this big scare Joe began to eat. His gut was ravaged. Either he had chronic diarrhea or would be in the ER for impacted bowels. One rainy day I heard a loud crashing noise. Joe was heading out of the back door in his wheelchair, loaded with tools. He had flipped the wheelchair over, landing hard on his back and the back of his head. The wheelchair was trashed, with both handles broken off. He said that he did not need to go to the hospital. I gave him some pain meds and he went to bed. The next day I was scheduled to work at the gallery in Sonoma where I show my jewelry. When B arrived in the morning I related the incident of the day before, telling her that under no circumstances should Joe be moved or put into a car. Later that afternoon I got a call from B. She told me that she had called Kaiser and — somehow — had scheduled an MRI for Joe. She was calling from the hospital. Asking her why she had ignored my specific instructions, she avoided the question and hung up. That night, two couples in our neighborhood — old friends of Joe's — had planned to come over and make dinner for us. They told me that dinner would be ready when I got home from work. Arriving home I saw that a beautiful table had been set and delicious smells were wafting through the house, from dinner bubbling on the stove. Joe and B were not there. I

149

told our friends about the phone call from B and expressed how angry I was that she had ignored my instructions. Later, they arrived, with B bringing Joe in a borrowed wheelchair. He was too exhausted to eat and B did not apologize.

Joe's primary care physician spoke with him about going to an assisted living facility where he could receive constant care. Taking care of everything had gone far beyond what a caregiver and myself were capable of handling. On 1/1/15, his doctor ordered that Joe be sent to a skilled nursing facility in Petaluma. Medicare had ordered the move and I had no say in this. It was not a facility that I would have chosen, but — according to Joe's doctor — was the only open bed in a place appropriate for his medical needs. The administrator explained to me that Medicare will only pay for a maximum of twenty days in skilled nursing, and that he would be leaving at the end of that time period. Again, I made daily visits with clean clothes during his stay. He was barely lucid and had completely stopped eating unless I brought him a milkshake. Each night when I came home, I went to the computer to send out an update to friends and family, as had been my habit all along. As usual, certain members of his family gave me grief, saying that I must be withholding information from them, instead of thanking me for the update. There was not much new to report, but I mentioned that they would be doing rounds the next day. I heard back from C, Joe's co-worker — the step-granddaughter's ex-husband. He said that the two of them wanted to be present at rounds. I responded by saying that this was personal, between my husband, his doctor and myself. Later that evening I listened to a phone message from C, who sounded very riled up. He said, "We'll be there whether you like it or not and there will be a scene!" The next morning early, I arranged for a meeting with the administrator of the facility, playing back the message for her. After listening to the message she told me, "Usually these things don't amount to much. But we will be prepared to call in the police to restrain hysterical family members if necessary." Joe was in a four-bed room, each patient separated only by curtains. There was not much space around each bed. Along with the four staff members, were myself, my sister-in-law and Bobby — who had come to lend me support — plus C and L. We were packed around the bed like sardines. Nothing of any medical importance came up during this brief meeting. I breathed a sigh of relief, and the troublemakers went home. Afterward, Joe commented on the fact that having "all those people" around him was disrespectful and upsetting. He would have anxiety attacks in crowds. That night I listened to a phone message from Joe, which came late at night. His voice was very weak and of course, his speech being so slurred, it was difficult to understand. But what he said was, "Babe, this is the last time you will ever hear from me because I am going to die tonight." Calling the facility to report the message and ask that they closely monitor him, I drove there as soon as it was light. He was still alive, but just barely. I was called to the office to sign paperwork, authorizing a transfer back to Kaiser. That night, after dark I received a call telling me that Joe was in an ambulance on his way back to Kaiser. Asking my sister-in-law to accompany me, we drove to the ER, arriving exactly at the same moment that they were bringing Joe in. No sooner than we had arrived, a nurse came in to tell me that there was a telephone call. It was C, telling me, "My mom's friend has a son on the same floor as Joe, so when she saw him being taken out on a gurney, she asked the ambulance driver where they were taking him." I just couldn't believe it. This was way beyond meddling. When he said that he planned to come right over I informed the nurse's station not to allow any visitors that night. C was infuriated. My poor husband was completely exhausted and confused and it was late. The next day, he was informed that he would only have a few days left to live.

Joseph had some friends from church, a husband and wife named Joe and Monica. They owned a care home in Kenwood that I had not even known existed. Joseph had spoken with these folks at church and told them that he wanted to be transferred to their facility for care. They, in turn, contacted me to discuss Joe's wishes. Once I had confirmed with my husband that these were indeed his specific wishes, they came to our house with the necessary documentation to allow the transfer. The paperwork was then confirmed with Kaiser and a medical equipment company was scheduled to deliver a bed and other necessary equipment. Then I attempted to sleep, completely exhausted — at the breaking point. The next morning while waiting to hear that Joe had been delivered safely to the care home in Kenwood, I received a call from a lady who identified herself as a social worker. She told me that I had better get right over to Kaiser because, "There is a real scene going on here in your husband's room."

Arriving at the big sliding glass doors of the entry to the hospital, I was met by L, Joe's stepbrother's daughter, accompanied by her children. To say that she appeared hysterical would be an understatement. "Why are you sending my uncle off to die?" The kids were glaring at me as if I were the devil incarnate. Trying to explain that I was following my husband's express wishes, she came unglued — crying and arguing with me. We went upstairs to his room, where there was indeed a noisy scene transpiring. There was L, the step-granddaughter, and B the kooky caregiver who was no longer in our employ — wearing her badge — along with the social worker. L and B were carrying on, pointing at me, loudly telling Joe, "She is sending you off to die!" Joseph was clearly agitated. L was sitting very close to him and shouting right in his face. Trying to explain to the social worker the plan that Joe had himself conceived, we then asked poor Joe and he started lamenting, "Call my lawyer." The social worker was flummoxed and asked me how we should proceed. In consideration of the total insanity going on around me I said, "Let's bring him home with hospice."

There was a lot of work to be done when I got home from the hospital. A call to Joe's friends at the care home was the first priority. They had spent hours on his paperwork, setting up the transfer with Kaiser and were naturally annoyed by the news that he would not be coming after all. The medical equipment had already been delivered there. A call was necessary to have it all picked up and re-delivered to our house. In consideration of the fact that our former caregiver B, had now clearly aligned herself with the hysterical relatives, I had to make sure that she would not be sent back to us. The new agency I called, sent a representative over within a few hours to interview me and inspect the premises. They set up a twenty-four-hour, three-shift schedule of caregivers. Out of curiosity, I asked if B was also an employee at that agency. It turned out that she was. I requested that she not be included as an employee for us. I didn't mention what had happened with her at the hospital. Hospice called to discuss everything in preparation for their visit. When I explained the ongoing situation with the step-granddaughter, arriving without calling and her propensity to go around to every door, testing locks — coming in, without knocking or ringing the bell, any time she felt like it, even though I made numerous requests that she cease and desist — they were horrified. I will never forget what one of the hospice nurses told me, "You have a dying person here. This is not a circus and you do not have a revolving door." She highly advised that I write up house rules and post them conspicuously on the doors — "Do not forget to list any unauthorized areas." I did this, stating that anyone who wanted to visit should first call for an appointment and that only two people at a time should be at the bedside for a visit as was Joe's request. In addition, I stated that Joe's office was off limits, as well as my bedroom and bathroom. These instructions were taped to both doors on the front of the house. My big mistake — I did not put them on either the side or back doors.

The following morning everything happened at once. Bright and early, the medical equipment was delivered and installed. The bed needed fresh linens. No sooner than the bed was made, both the ambulance bringing Joe and the new first-shift caregiver arrived. We introduced them, got him into bed and then I went over the house rules with her. She told me that she understood and agreed not to let anyone in without an appointment.

153

Numerous nurses from hospice, each with different responsibilities, came throughout the day. Endless paperwork and hospice regulations were signed and discussed. Finally, the medications were laid out and specific instructions were outlined. Each time any medication was administered it was to be noted, along with the time, on one of their forms. The stronger drugs were given to me in a little safe, which I was instructed to hide. By that afternoon, every surface in my living room was covered with paperwork and medicine. All of this had taken the better part of the day. At three PM, the final nurse who spoke to me said that her job was to make sure I would be able handle all of this and didn't fall apart. She wanted to know how I planned to take care of myself? Looking at my watch, I was glad to tell her that I had a massage scheduled for three-thirty in the art studio. She was thrilled and said that she could leave knowing that I would be ok. Going into the bedroom, I kissed Joseph and let Betty, the new caregiver, know that I would be close by and back in an hour. She knew that there were no visits scheduled for Joe. Anticipating a quiet hour of much-needed relaxation, I went out of the back door and down the driveway to meet the massage guy. My big mistake: I did not remember to lock the back door behind me.

Tim, the massage guy, was telling me that "lots of cars" were speeding up the driveway. But secure in the knowledge that notes were posted on the locked doors and Betty was in charge, everything would be fine. I tried to enjoy the massage. An hour later, looking up at the house I saw seven or eight cars parked, not in the driveway, but alongside the house. Coming in through the back door, I saw L and B and numerous of Joe's relatives sitting around in the living room, hanging out and reading his medical paperwork. No one would make eye contact with me. I couldn't believe my eyes. They had not called to say that they were coming and had come in through the back door! The signs on the front doors had been taken down. Running down the hall to our bedroom, I found Joe's surly attorney standing beside the hospital bed, clutching a handful of our bank statements. C and one of Joe's nephews were also there, all guiltily reading paperwork taken from our office. They wouldn't make eye contact with me either. My head was spinning! The attorney told me that L had called him and the rest of the people and asked them to meet her at our house. But no call was made to me and Joe told me later, that no one had called him. Then the rest of the crowd began to filter into the bedroom. At this point, I flipped out and asked them all to leave. Poor Betty felt terrible, telling me that they had rushed in through the back door before she had a chance to stop them. As they were all driving away, both my husband and I spontaneously burst into tears. He asked me to get into bed with him. He had lost so much weight that it was not even a tight squeeze. Lying there, rocking each other ,he said, "You mean everything in the world to me, none of the rest of this really matters." Betty, sitting nearby, tearfully witnessed the entire thing. We agreed that I should have a lock put on the office door in the morning.

I woke up at five AM, uncomfortable in the knowledge that workers I had never met, were moving around in my house, changing shifts. Going straight in to monitor Joe's breathing, the first thing I saw was crazy B, sitting in the corner, wearing a t-shirt from the current caregiving agency. Betty told me that B had come in the dark to the back bedroom door and demanded to be admitted, claiming that the agency had sent her. Asking B to follow me to the kitchen, I told her that she would have to leave. Arguing that she would not go, I threatened to call the sheriff. She continued to argue and finally left. Standing outside next to her car, she was shouting into her phone. Meanwhile, I called the agency, waking up the owner, who assured me that they had not sent B. She put her husband on the speakerphone. He was livid and said that her behavior was "completely unacceptable." She also told me something I had not been aware of prior to our conversation: Caregivers who were not scheduled and on the clock were forbidden to see their clients outside of the work environment. B had been hanging out for weeks, wearing her badge, at the skilled nursing facility and at Kaiser. This, I was told, was in itself, grounds for dismissal from any caregiving agency. Everything had spun completely out of control. Later that morning, after a locksmith had come and gone, L actually called and asked if she and C could come to see Joe. I had reported the home invasion incident to hospice, telling them what time these two troublemakers planned to make their visit. Hospice sent a social worker to sit with me and wait for their arrival. L was furious that she was required to ring the doorbell. When I opened the door, she rushed right past me, straight to the office and began shaking the door. She could see Joe, lying in his hospital bed at the end of the hallway in a near-death state and yet she began screaming shrilly at the top of her lungs, "Gramp, Nancy put a lock on the office door!" The social worker was appalled and said that now she was able to understand the weird reports that were coming in about this case. Following L down the hall, standing quietly behind her, I heard her ask Betty if I were responsible for Joe's current condition. She wanted to know if I had been over-medicating him? Because each medication delivery was notated, Betty assured L that this could not be true. In fact, I called the hospice office each time Joe felt like he was in need of any additional medication — to ask permission before giving it to him. All of L's efforts thwarted, because she could not get into Joe's office and help herself to whatever she wanted, or accuse me of harming my husband, she and C soon left after loudly berating me. By the following morning, Joseph was in a non-responsive state, dying. The attorney called to say that he wanted to come. Relating Joe's current condition and attempting to discourage him — "shouldn't we just give him some peace?" — he insisted that he would come. Apparently he did not believe me, because he arrogantly strode past me — in his typical unfriendly manner — down the hall to the bedroom, carrying an overstuffed briefcase. I didn't bother to follow him. He quickly and angrily departed without saying goodbye, exhibiting no compassion or remorse.

Joe remained in a peaceful, non-responsive state until the

following morning when he ultimately passed away, with Betty and myself at his bedside. The hospice regulations state, that they must be contacted within so many minutes of a person's death. One of their nurses arrived immediately to collect and measure all remaining medications. She warned me that someone had called them to report that I was responsible for having over-medicated my husband. Telling me not to worry she assured me that the remaining medications checked out perfectly with the notations. Who would act like this in the face of death? For many months following this unnecessary stress, I had violent, hideous nightmares and was diagnosed with stomach ulcers and post-traumatic stress disorder.

Prior to Emma's death, plans had been arranged for Joseph's funeral. He was to be entombed next to her at the local Catholic cemetery. One of his trusts had a payment provision for this. Being a prominent man, we knew that many people from the community and his church would want to attend his funeral. Joe and I had discussed this issue at length in the weeks preceding his death, so that I could be very clear about his wishes. His primary request was that the mass be said in his home church in Oakmont. In recent weeks he had visited with a local couple who provided regular catering at the church parish center. Choosing the specific menu he desired for the luncheon, which would take place following his funeral, his caterer friend Laura told me that — true to form — "Joe knew exactly what he wanted."

Entering the mortuary, carrying a suit of Joseph's clothes on a hanger, I experienced a feeling of dread. Going through the motions for the preparation of my husband's funeral was exhausting and naturally unpleasant, but I continued on, administering his wishes. The funeral director had reason to call me on several occasions within the next few days. Apparently, L making a huffy visit, identified herself as Joe's daughter and made various demands. Since the mortuary was providing the death certificates, the director knew that Joseph had no children and was confused as to why she would lie? I asked him to comply with any of her wishes as best he could.

At the Catholic Church, I met with Joe's parish priest and Blanche, the funeral coordinator, who assisted me with the planning of the mass. A spate of deaths with various parishioners of the church had occurred that same week and it was booked with funerals, causing a delay in our scheduling. C and L, along with a few of Joe's relatives were very upset by this dilemma, calling the parish center to complain. So many of their irate calls were received that, finally the parish center called me. Joe's priest requested that I contact the bothersome callers and ask them to stop contacting the parish center. I asked C to please let Joe rest in peace.

A Catholic funeral mass is a very complex series of ritualized events. It would be my job, with help from the priests, to structure the various portions of the mass — organize readers, hire musicians, select and order flowers, as well as choosing the pallbearers and have the mass booklet printed — a project which my friend Joan thankfully undertook and completed. All of this, of course, needed to be coordinated with the director of the mortuary. In addition, Preston Smith and his wife Lois, friends of Joe's who had, for several months, been filming a wine-industry documentary on Joe, hoping to complete it before his death, kindly offered to screen the film during the luncheon following the funeral mass.

The church was packed to overflowing with some three hundred and fifty people. The mass was very beautiful, with Joe's dear friend Fr. Patrick Leslie presiding. Right up until minutes prior to the funeral, L stood outside the doors of the church, contentiously arguing with Blanche. She and another family member insisted on bringing a large photo of Emma and a photo collage of their families inside, to be placed by the casket.

Finally, Blanche convinced them to take the photos next door to the parish center. At the end of the funeral mass, while following the casket out to be placed in the hearse, I encountered the parish priest. He gave me a big hug and whispered in my ear, "I've really got to hand it to you. I don't know how you have managed to put up with Joe's family."

Afterword
Stigma and Shame

On July 14, 2016, I sent off an email to Shirlee Zane, Sonoma County Board of Supervisors, District 3:

Topic: Constituent Matter
Subject: Mental Health
Message: Ms. Zane, I am in the process of writing my memoir and am interviewing various people on issues related to my life – one being that my late husband was bipolar and the negativity and stigmas I encountered in attempts to find help for him, a prominent man – within his family, business and church in Sonoma County. Would you grant me a short office visit and share your views?

In the biography section on her web site list, Ms. Zane's highest priorities are listed as, "housing, homelessness, environmental and health and public safety." Articles in the Santa Rosa Press Democrat have frequently discussed her fervor on the issue of mental health. Because she had been so outspoken on the issues of timely mental health treatment for all – and the stigma and shame associated with mental health issues – I felt compelled to meet her. Fully aware of the fact that our public servants are well known to have overbooked schedules, I honestly did not expect to hear back from her office. A few months later, much to my surprise I was scheduled into a meeting with her at her county center office, eagerly anticipating the opportunity to hear what she would have to say. Shirlee's husband Peter, who had made a previous suicide attempt, had finally taken his own life after being denied timely psychiatric treatment at Kaiser Permanente. Although Peter was being monitored for anxiety treatment, Shirlee feels that he was "dramatically undertreated ... and with little or no follow-up." She went on to discuss the differences in acceptance and treatment for physical ailments as opposed to mental health ailments, for which patients are "grossly undertreated, discriminated against and seemingly must fight to obtain," and went on to say, "If there is a deliberate model that could deliver better mental health treatment, it would be a model like Kaiser." Although the Mental Health Parity and Addiction Equality Act was passed in 2008, substance abuse was being treated, but mental health was still being stigmatized and disrespected by insurers. CMS, the organization responsible for enforcing Medicaid and Medicare parity within government health services, had not yet seen any lawsuits against insurers for not achieving parity, although there had been many wrongful death cases. In November 2015, Shirlee and Patrick J. Kennedy, along with Darryl Steinberg, the California Senate President *pro tempore*, collaborated on a second CA state system strike — an indefinite strike — after Shirlee suggested to Kaiser that they needed to hire additional therapists to help equalize the therapist/patient caseload systems, with the goal that all patients could be assured of receiving treatment within a two week period after being seen or diagnosed by their doctor. Instead of fighting, Kaiser settled that day. At the end of our interview, Shirlee told me, "People often ask me the cause of my husband's death and I always say, it was caused by depression."

A few days prior to my meeting with Shirlee, the Santa Rosa Press Democrat published an article, entitled *Clinton Unveils Mental Health Plan To End Stigma and Shame*. The article stated that Hillary Clinton's plan "would attempt to integrate the nation's health care system, to create a more seamless way of providing both medical and mental health treatment to patients."

During the course of our meeting, Shirlee encouraged me to

read Patrick J. Kennedy's 2015 memoir, *A Common Struggle — A Personal Journey Through the Past and Future of Mental Illness and Addiction*. I found Patrick's book to be an absolute treasure trove of information. He relates the numerous governmental attempts made to pass into law, reasonable parity/equity of insurance coverage for mental health, as well as physical health. Patrick, throughout his book, refers instead of mental health, to "brain health." Son of the late US Senator, Edward 'Ted' Kennedy and nephew of the late President of the United States, John F. Kennedy, Patrick has spent much of his lifetime attempting to lift the "veil of secrecy" which surrounds the extensive and famous Kennedy clan. Alcoholism was a prevalent problem within his family and Patrick says, "We had to decide: would we be true to ourselves or true to the family code of silence?" His story is largely concerned with his own "coming out" to his constituency, his family and the general public about his bipolar disorder and subsequent addiction to prescription drugs. He was forced to deny his bipolarity, not only from himself, but also from everyone he encountered throughout his childhood, formative school years and political history. Consequently — not surprisingly — he self-medicated and became a drug addict at a very young age. Both Patrick and his mother Joan spent countless years of their lives in therapy and at treatment centers. Not the first members of his family to have suffered from these types of illnesses, he says that there are no cures for this type of chronic illness often associated with a genetic risk. "Only medical treatments, AA meetings, research, spirituality along with hope and belief in a common struggle, can help the sufferer of this type of brain disease." In addition, he states that each sector of the medical community treating mental illness and/or addiction is "challenged, underfunded and discriminated against … in their attempts to overcome stereotypes, prejudice and marginalization."

In the summer of 1962, Patrick's aunt, Eunice Shriver created a small summer camp for children with disabilities — including her niece Rosemary — in her backyard in Potomac, Maryland. This camp eventually grew into what we now know as the Special Olympics.

In 1963 JFK delivered his landmark speech, "A Special

Message to the Congress on Mental Illness and Mental Retardation." This was the first time that this topic had been discussed in public by a world leader.

In 1965 a Medicaid law, the "IMD Exclusion" was established to hasten the emptying of hospitals housing more than 51% of mentally ill patients and to prevent them from receiving Medicaid reimbursements. Patrick states that, "Today this outdated law just makes modern inpatient facilities all but economically unfeasible, leaving the nation with a serious shortage of hospital beds for patients with mental illness."

In 1996, Patrick helped pass a federal parity law, which was enacted and proved to be largely inefficient. Carrying the Kennedy torch for equality, he continued on his quest for mental health parity into the year 2000 and beyond, along with his mentor — and AA sponsor — Jim Ramstad, drafting a bill in the house, which they hoped would be a "full civil rights act for all brain disorders." According to Patrick, "the real issue of parity was basically state and local — it was about holding their local private health insurance providers accountable using either the federal law or their state law ... and accessing the enforcement power of state insurance commissioners and state attorneys general."

In 1999 the Clinton administration continued the fight for mental health parity.

When President Barack Obama included mental health protections in his Affordable Care Act, Patrick says that he understood how Mr. Obama had to juggle the needs of the people, with those of the powerful insurance companies whose support was needed to pass the landmark bill. "A lot of us were concerned the administration had not been focused enough on the epidemic of suicides, overdoses and addiction, and that it was dragging its feet on full implementation of mental health parity." In a White House speech, President Obama, praising Patrick for his determination to pass his bill was quoted as saying, "It's not enough to help more Americans seek treatment — we also have to make sure that the treatment is there when they're ready to seek it."

Still today, no final mental health parity rules have been

164

established.

On February 23, 2016, Patrick J. Kennedy — a former Rhode Island congressman and Dr. David Satcher — U.S. Surgeon General called on both Democrats and Republicans to stand together and "Rally Behind a New Vision." Patrick Kennedy firmly believes, "The State of the Union in Mental Health and Addiction is one of great promise, but it is going to take all of us working together to realize its full potential. The goal is to improve lives and transform the broken healthcare system." Dr. Satcher has stated, "We must work at the state and national level to ensure that health equity is a top concern, and access to healthcare for low-income populations is protected and expanded. It is essential that we secure solutions directed at filling the gaps that currently exist in the system."

In my own life, I feel sure that if my husband had not been in denial about his own and his various family members' mental health issues because of stigma and shame, he might have asked for help at some point in his life. I know that it was extremely difficult for him to appear as Jovial Joe in public. He was a man's man, loving to hang out, overeating, and drinking with his nonjudgmental buddies. But often he would return from random public events — especially after having too much to drink — agitated and having an anxiety attack, sometimes even crying. His release mechanism was quick escape. Without a word to anyone, no matter what the consequences, he would literally run to his car and flee. He definitely had a tendency to self-medicate, especially at night.

In retrospect, our life and marriage could have been so very different if he had been taking helpful medications appropriately prescribed by a psychiatrist, instead of waiting until after having had a stroke to be properly diagnosed.

165

Photo Gallery

Nancy on horse 1952

1965 San Rafael High School

Nancy and Al 1967

168

Walking Down the Aisle 1967

Sons of Champlin 1967 (courtesy Joel Selvin)

169

Spinning in Woodacre 1972

Nancy and Bill 1973

New parents 1974

Playing with Aura

Happy Mom

Barclay family 1978

Nancy modeling shirt

Danskin© ad 1978

Nancy and Joe Wedding Day 2004

Joe Martin

Nancy, Joe, Amigo & Taffy
St. Francis Winery Blessing of the Animals 2009

About the Author

Nancy J. Martin was born in San Francisco, raised in Marin County and migrated north to the Valley of the Moon, where she has resided since 1976.

Nancy & Milagro 2008